"The vast majority of teachers are passionate about their work; Evelein and Korthagen describe how to tap this passion in order to sustain them in their important work. This project is exciting and full of potential for me as a teacher mentor."

—Paul McCormick, University of Pennsylvania Graduate School of Education, USA

"This book is at the forefront of the field. As a 'workbook' it takes theory and practice, moulds them together in useable ways, and makes it possible for a teacher to not only make sense of the ideas but be capable of leading their development in classroom practice."

—John Loughran, Monash University, Australia

"This is a unique collection that will enhance the work of all who aspire to become reflective practitioners."

—Tom Russell, Queen's University, Canada

Practicing Core Reflection features 78 concrete educational activities and exercises based on research. These can be used individually and in groups to support "teaching and learning from within." Core Reflection is an approach focused on people's personal strengths and on using practical strategies to overcome obstacles to the enactment of these strengths. This approach has been used in many contexts all over the world and has shown great promise in helping to re-chart the course for education and to re-think its purpose in global and democratic societies. Additional tools (Cards, Figures, Tables, Forms in a printable PDF format) are provided on a separate website (www.routledge.com/9780415819961).

Building on the theoretical foundations established in Korthagen, Kim, and Green's *Teaching and Learning from Within: A Core Reflection Approach to Quality and Inspiration in Education*, this companion volume can be used together with it or on its own. Either way it engages educators in exploring what it means to bring out the best in oneself, in students, in colleagues, and others and to become more natural and authentic role models for promoting the excitement of learning with students—a critically significant project if education is to realize new levels of possibility and potential.

Frits G. Evelein is an expert in education and art. He held various positions as a professor in teacher education at Utrecht University in the Netherlands, and in music and arts education at Codarts University of Performing Arts in Rotterdam. Currently he is involved in developing innovations in education and art.

Fred A. J. Korthagen is emeritus professor of education at Utrecht University in the Netherlands. In 2000 and in 2006 he received the Exemplary Research in Teaching and Teacher Education Award from the Teaching and Teacher Education division of AERA. In 2009 he received the Distinguished Research Award from the Association of Teacher Educators.

Susan Schüller

Practicing Core Reflection

Activities and Lessons for Teaching and Learning from Within

Frits G. Evelein and Fred A. J. Korthagen

 Routledge
Taylor & Francis Group

NEW YORK AND LONDON

First published 2015
by Routledge
711 Third Avenue, New York, NY 10017

and by Routledge
2 Park Square, Milton Park, Abingdon, Oxon OX14 4RN

Routledge is an imprint of the Taylor & Francis Group, an informa business

© 2015 Taylor & Francis

The right of Frits G. Evelein and Fred A. J. Korthagen to be identified as author of this work has been asserted by them in accordance with sections 77 and 78 of the Copyright, Designs and Patents Act 1988.

All rights reserved. No part of this book may be reprinted or reproduced or utilized in any form or by any electronic, mechanical, or other means, now known or hereafter invented, including photocopying and recording, or in any information storage or retrieval system, without permission in writing from the publishers.

Trademark notice: Product or corporate names may be trademarks or registered trademarks, and are used only for identification and explanation without intent to infringe.

Library of Congress Cataloging-in-Publication Data
Evelein, Frits G.
  Practicing core reflection : activities and lessons for teaching and learning from within / Frits G. Evelein, Fred A. J. Korthagen.
    pages cm
  Includes bibliographical references and index.
  1. Reflective teaching. 2. Reflective learning. 3. Critical thinking—Study and teaching—Activity programs. 4. Teachers—In-service training. I. Korthagen, Fred A. J., 1949– II. Title.
  LB1025.3.E867 2014
  371.102—dc23
  2014003107

ISBN: 978-0-415-81995-4 (hbk)
ISBN: 978-0-415-81996-1 (pbk)
ISBN: 978-0-203-76471-8 (ebk)

Typeset in Stone Serif
by Apex CoVantage, LLC

Printed and bound in the United States of America by Publishers Graphics, LLC on sustainably sourced paper.

Contents

Preface

This is a book for everyone who works in education. It guides you on a journey in which you will explore and manifest your personal qualities and talents more fully. You may be familiar with those situations in which you feel inspired and where everything you do seems successful. At other moments, however, you may become blocked or frustrated by your endeavor, thus leading you to doubt yourself. Are these differences simply part of life or can you influence what happens? Is it possible to work with more pleasure and at the same time be more effective?

This book offers a positive answer to these questions. The activities that are presented will help you experience your inner potential more fully. They also show how you can overcome the obstacles you encounter. This can help you flourish as a professional while being more deeply connected with others.

Through various activities and exercises you will start a journey of finding your inner source of quality, creativity, energy, and inspiration. You will tap into the potential that lies waiting inside and you will discover how you can use this potential more optimally. Problems and challenges that you encounter can then become invitations for development and growth.

This book is based on many years of experience with coaching and training people in all kinds of organizations, but most of all on our work with people in education. We have found that teachers or other professionals in education who feel stuck can suddenly 'get into flow' by using relatively simple, but powerful principles. We also discovered that this often leads to enduring transformations in which a person's strengths and their profession become intertwined in exciting new ways. In the book *Teaching and learning from within* (Korthagen, Kim, & Greene, 2013), we described these experiences and the underlying theory. The approach that we use is called *core reflection* and aims at strengthening the unity among all layers of the personal and the professional dimensions.

As more and more people became fascinated by the practical applications of core reflection, we decided to write the book you are now reading. It is a valuable guidebook for all those working in education: beginning and experienced teachers, coaches, supervisors, collaborating teachers, school principals, superintendents, teacher educators, and student teachers who desire to become successful professionals.

Our approach to professional development is somewhat different from most views. It has become common to list standards and competencies in attempts to capture the essence of professional performance in fixed frameworks, measurable criteria, and behavioral protocols. However, concerns are growing that this perspective is not very helpful for bringing out the best in people. People's potential tends to become cramped or stifled when they feel overly restricted by external mandates. What is often overlooked is that professionals can only flourish if they can use their personal qualities in their work, if they can stay true to who they are. In other words, lists of standards or competencies are certainly important and sometimes informative, but they can only contribute to professional development if, first of all, personal strengths are taken seriously as the starting point for developing effective behavior.

Each chapter of this book is focused on a specific theme. Based on these themes, we clarify what teaching and learning from within can mean for your daily practice. We do so by offering powerful activities that link to daily practices. We also briefly discuss the underlying theory for each theme. This helps you develop fresh insights and new possibilities for effective behavior. Although we mainly focus on the professional context, much of what you will learn can also be applied to your personal life.

Although this is first and foremost a practical book, at the end of each chapter we discuss the relevant academic knowledge and research base on which the chapter was built. Additionally, in the first and the last chapters we share practical guidelines for how to make optimal use of this book: individually, in professional teams or groups, and in training or coaching settings.

This book was first published in Dutch. During the writing process many people have supported and inspired us. most of all the inspiring researchers working on self-determination theory and within positive psychology, our colleagues with whom we developed the core reflection approach, and the numerous participants in the educational programs, workshops, and training courses we have provided.

In particular, we thank Mariska Evelein for her translation of this book into English. We are grateful to our US colleagues Younghee Kim and William Greene for their detailed comments and inspiring suggestions on the draft version of the present book. Their passion for spreading the core reflection approach in the US has touched us and has been an important incentive for translating this book. We thank Naomi Silverman at Routledge for her trust in the ambition we have for this book.

Note

If this book creates the wish to go deeper and learn more about the core reflection approach and really integrate it in one's daily practices, the reader may find that there are limits to learning to use core reflection in its full depth from a book. It might then be helpful to follow a brief course or training workshop in core reflection. If you want to know more about core reflection training or workshops, visit the website at www.korthagen.nl or contact the authors (f.g.evelein@gmail.com or fred@korthagen.nl).

1 Working From your Inner Core

An Outline

Jim has just started his first teaching job. He still feels young and inexperienced when dealing with students, so he has a somewhat hesitant attitude. In the classroom he tries to do his best but seems a bit withdrawn. However, he gradually notices that the students like his openness and his experiments with a more creative approach. Slowly, he puts more creativity into his lessons and instructional methods. The students love it.

This book is for all people working in education who want to realize their full potential and to enjoy their work. It is very suited for teachers and other professionals who are experienced and good at their work but who feel they could benefit from further professional development, and for those in structured professional development programs. This book is all about teaching and learning from within, using all of your strengths and talents. Finding this core potential inside yourself and using it in your work can be very beneficial to all current or future roles you might have in education.

In the example above, we see how Jim is initially quite withdrawn in his teaching. But he recognizes quickly that he has a lot to offer. He shows that he has many fresh ideas which are appreciated by the students. His creativity shows up when it comes to designing new ways of working, a personal quality making him a strong professional. Slowly, he also starts utilizing another quality, that of courage; the courage to be who he is and to use what he has to offer, for example his creativity. This is a personal quality he possessed before but did not use. He starts using it more, and this earns him more appreciation from his students.

At the core of this book is the understanding that many people have important personal qualities which they are not fully utilizing in their work. Often much more is possible than is realized. It is useful to start with the question: Do you know your core qualities and talents and can you apply them? Or are you blocked in doing this? If so, can you let go of these blocks and optimally apply your qualities? Having an understanding of this helps enormously in developing yourself.

1 Introductory Activity: Reflection on Inspiration and Stagnation

This activity helps you to explore your core qualities.

Introductory Activity: Reflection on Inspiration and Stagnation

1-1	Think back on an inspiring situation at work.
2-1	How did you experience this situation? What did you do well? For example: were you persistent and precise, or did you interact well with others? Write down some of the words that reflect your strengths in this situation. We call these *core qualities*.
3-1	Now go back to a situation which was less pleasant, or one in which you were really stuck; one where you felt stagnated.
4-1	How did you experience this situation? What exactly made it difficult? See if there is also something inside yourself that made it hard. For example perhaps there was a belief system which came up, like "I cannot do this," "I am afraid to do this," "I am strange," "I don't want to do this." What effect did such a belief system have on you in this situation?
5-1	What is the difference between the inspired and stagnated situation? Are you applying different core qualities to each situation? Do you have different belief systems showing up in each situation?
6-1	What can you do to apply your core qualities (like the ones you used in the inspiring situation) in difficult situations? Think, for example, of clarity, trust, contact, precision, courage, humor, or passion.

In this book we will not only explain what it means to work from within, but will also help you to experience it. This book is, first of all, a practical handbook using activities to help you discover who you are and how you can apply your core qualities at work. How can you utilize your personal strengths so that you can be and remain inspired? How can you be most effective in your work?

The Possible Applications of This Book

This book is about professional development in education, but not just for one type of career. What we will be learning can be applied to all types of work and to many contexts. Many elements of this book can, for example, be utilized to improve your teaching, classroom management, and leadership but also for coaching and training, programs focused on professional development, career counselling, professional workshops, personal reflections, writing a portfolio or CV, etc.

An assumption underlying this book is that, ideally, professional and personal growth go hand in hand and that the combination of these two will help you find your own personal strengths, since the most powerful professionals are shaped by a strong connection between who they are and their professional behavior.

The Vision

We, the authors of this book, have been working with student teachers, experienced teachers, educational leaders, and people from many other backgrounds and professions. While doing this, we started to recognize how simple ideas and exercises can often have a huge impact on professional development. They can show people a very beneficial development route that they have never seen before. We have found that a lot of human potential is underutilized because people do not know what is possible. It is amazingly inspiring to see the dormant potential of a person suddenly take shape and be recognized. That is why this book aims to connect the personal and the professional.

We have also discovered that many misconceptions exist about this connection of the person and the profession. For example, often people's perception is that something is wrong with you if you look to others for support regarding a personal struggle at work or home. It is our belief, however, that asking for support is a great way to turn silver into gold. The most powerful people are the ones who realize that you never stop learning and that continuous development should be supported professionally.

Another misunderstanding is that 'working on yourself' is hard and will bring up traumatic experiences from your youth. This thought pattern seems to stem from a long-expired understanding dating back to the work of Freud, which stubbornly remains in our collective thinking. True, psychology has for a long time focused on finding and 'treating' youth traumas and wounds, but to a large degree this thinking has now been replaced by the concept of tapping into innate strengths and inner potential. Personal development has become an area of inspiration and joy and can lead to strong professional growth.

One of the authors of this book, Frits Evelein, is familiar with the world of music and music education. He has even made this his career. Art shows how using your own creative potential can sometimes lead to new developments, which you would never have thought possible. Art also shows that a playful and joyful attitude is important in this. Hence, working on your professional development does not have to be a serious and heavy experience. By play-fully exploring new elements that present themselves, you can discover new opportunities that seem unheard of. Just think about a group of musicians who come together to have fun and make music. They can create an enor-mous feeling of 'flow' and produce amazing music. Using the example of music, we may ask you: How are you going to make your music at work, and in doing so, have fun with others? The activities in this book give you many opportunities to discover more about this. Much more is possible than you can dream of; our traditional thought patterns about ourselves are often our biggest stumbling blocks.

Of course, sometimes it can also hurt to realize how you have slowly moved away from your core—from who you really are—and this can even bring up melancholic memories about the time you were an innocent child. These feelings are a normal part of learning to work and live according to your core. Most people who are looking to make more use of their talents and qualities will go through this process at some point; it is a major step toward working and living in agreement with who you are.

The Structure of This Book

Each chapter of this book is written around a specific theme connected to professional development. We base our writing on the latest scientific developments, because recently, much research has been done around this topic. Over the last decade, a lot has been learned about human potential, some of which is rediscovered knowledge which has existed for thousands of years and is now translated for our time. Completely new discoveries are also being made and have led to new theories that are directly applicable to professionals, and can have a big impact on your daily work.

Although this book is based on scientific research, this research is not our main or only focus in the chapters. Rather we start from the perspective of everyday personal experiences at work or gained during professional training activities. To support this, the first part of each chapter will describe the chapter theme from an everyday perspective and will contain one or more practical activities (like the activity above), which may help you to recognize the theme in your work situation, your training, or at home. They are called 'introductory activities' and are aimed at connecting your personal experiences with scientific concepts.

Following the practical introduction, each chapter contains a section called 'Further exploration.' This section will deepen your understanding of the ins and outs of the theme and is especially aimed at making the connection between you and your daily experiences at work. You can do these activities on your own, in groups of two, or four, or in a larger group.

Each chapter ends with a section called 'Scientific background,' in which we briefly reflect back on the chapter theme from a scientific perspective and help you find sources that support or deepen the theme of the chapter. Everything in this section will be referenced. These references could help you to find further information if you are looking for more detail. We will keep this section of each chapter short and concise, as we think the most valuable aspect of this book is the focus on experience and practical application. For anyone looking for more theoretical detail it is useful to know that the approach that lies at the core of this book is further developed in the theory of *core reflection*. This theory has been summarized in the book *Teaching and learning from within* (Korthagen, Kim, & Greene, 2013). This book also discusses a variety of practical applications of core reflection, as well as empirical studies on the resulting learning processes and learning outcomes in professionals. More background information and references to other publications and workshops can be found on www.korthagen.nl.

Finding Your Way Through the Activities

All of the activities in this book will help you to become aware of your own qualities and those of others, to strengthen those qualities, and to let go of blocks that may be limiting you. It would be possible to mix up the activities and use them in any order, but we think you would benefit from doing some

#	Example of question	Description of activity
1	How do I improve my focus and concentration?	Improving your focus (19, 20, 68), concentration, perception, and precision (9,12)
2	How do I recognize my own and others' qualities?	Recognizing core qualities (2, 3, 4, 5, 6, 7, 8) and learning to give feedback (14)
3	How do I limit myself in what I do?	How are you unconsciously limiting your own power (48, 60) and growth (29), and how can you change this (12, 53, 61, 62)?
4	What choices do I make (or not) and what are my dilemmas?	What choices do you make and why (25, 31, 34, 38, 39)? How do you deal with dilemmas (48, 49, 54)?
5	What are my ideals, what drives me, and what are my values?	Discover you ideals (36, 37), how they can stimulate your growth (38, 39), whether you are (un)faithful to them (40) and which values you apply (10).

Table 1.1   Examples of questions that the activities can help you with
See Chapter 10, Table 10.1 for a more detailed overview.

of the introductory activities first. These are clearly indicated at the start of each chapter. They are short, stand-alone activities to help you understand an aspect of the theme. The different aspects will be expanded on in the rest of the chapter.

We also think that you would benefit from reading and practicing with concrete personal experiences and questions in mind, arising from your experiences at work or in training settings. In this way, you can use your work or training to feed your qualities. To support you in this, Table 1.1 lists some themes or questions people often have from professional experience, training, or their private life. For each theme, we list some activities from the book that can help you deal with the problem related to the theme. A larger overview of themes and related activities is given in Chapter 10 (Table 10.1).

The Structure of the Activities

Although the activities can be partly performed on your own, they are more beneficial when done in pairs, teams of four, or a large group. Each part of every activity indicates how many people it is designed for. An activity could, for example, have the following structure:

Example structure of an activity

Goal: This describes the goal of the activity. **Materials:** Here we indicate which materials are best for you to use. Most of the materials are included in a pdf format on the website: www.routledge.com/9780415819961	1-1	This is part 1 of the activity. The second number—here number 1—indicates that it is designed for an individual on their own, and this is also indicated by the pale grey tint. If you are working through this book on your own, you can decide to focus only on these parts of the activities. We ask you to document your insights clearly when doing an activity. Most of the time we will ask you to write something down.
	2-2	This is part 2 of the activity. The second number—here the number 2—indicates it should be done in pairs.
	3-G	This is part 3 of the activity. The letter G indicates it is a group activity with interaction between all the members of the pairs combined. This group can be guided by a teacher or coach, but we imagine that some groups will be able to do an activity on their own.
	4-1	This is part 4. Another example of an individual activity.
	5-2	Part 5 is designed for a pair.
	6-4	Part 6 is designed for teams of 4, for example formed by combining two pairs of part 5.
	7-G	Part 7 is again a group activity.

In Chapter 10, more descriptions are given on how to use the activities, how to form pairs or teams, and how to work with larger groups.

Materials for the Activities

Linked to this book are many materials and tools for the activities. They can be found on the website at: www.routledge.com/9780415819961. Click on the eResource tab for access to the material. These tools are:

1. *Cards*: You can print a pdf of all cards that are used for the activities. Cut the cards along the lines, and if you use the cards often (e.g. if you work with many groups) you can laminate the page before cutting out the cards. Each set of cards can be held together with an elastic band.
2. *Figures*: Figures from this book.

3. *Tables:* Tables from this book.
4. *Forms:* The forms are also available on the website.

NOTE: Throughout the book, the URL for the website is designated with the symbol @.

The Topics of the Chapters

We will now give a brief outline of all the chapters.

Chapter 2 is called *Tapping into the Power of Your Core Qualities*. Examples of core qualities are: precision, endurance, courage, enthusiasm, etc. Every person has many qualities, which together form an important 'inner potential.' The question is how you can make optimal use of this potential. We show how recent developments in the field of psychology about the core qualities of people can answer this question. In this chapter you will, for example, make your own 'core quality profile.'

Chapter 3 is called *Using Three Information Channels: Thinking, feeling, and wanting*. Although there is a strong focus on thinking in our society, we see people as beings that also have feelings, needs, and desires. In particular, the ability to feel and want something has enormous power when it comes to professional development, but for a long time this has not been recognized in many educational and professional contexts. This chapter focuses on restoring the balance between the channels of thinking, feeling, and wanting and will let you experience the power of this. We will focus on how you can fine-tune these channels. Finally, this chapter will paint a picture of a vision in which personal development focuses on 'the whole person.'

Chapter 4 is titled: *Using the Power of Your Desires and Ideals*. Desires and ideals indicate what it is that you want, what it is that drives you, and what your values and wishes are at work and in your personal development. Research into the basic psychological needs of people shows that each person is born with the desire to control the direction of their life (the need for autonomy), to be able to deal with the demands of their environment (the need for competence), and the desire to have meaningful relationships with other people (the need for relatedness). These desires represent huge powers which can be positively harnessed. When you gain a better understanding of how these processes work and how they can make you stronger in your job, things will become easier, and you can achieve more with less energy.

This brings us to the theme of Chapter 5: *Going With the Flow*. This chapter focuses on the possibility that everything 'flows' and seems to go smoothly. If you are 'in flow,' you are completely focused on the here and now and your qualities become clearly visible. Important research findings about flow can help you in your daily work. Some people think it is all a coincidence when they are in a situation of flow, but we will show that you can improve the chance of creating flow, and we will help you find out how to do this in your own situation.

A focus on the positive aspects of work is great, but unfortunately people also continuously run up against struggles in which there is no flow at all. They encounter small or large problems. What happens is that in situations like these, we often create negative belief systems about ourselves, the world, and others.

We will look at this in more detail in Chapter 6, which has as a theme: *Letting Go of Limitations*. In this chapter we will also help you look at your basic response patterns when being confronted with problems. Do you fight, take flight, or freeze? Can you change these patterns?

Chapter 7 is called *Connecting the Aspects of Your Personality*. People are complex beings who act, feel, think, desire, and have belief systems and self-images. We also experience a sort of timeless essence inside, which in this book we call 'the core.' All of these different aspects are important. In this chapter you will discover which role these various aspects of your personality play, and how in some situations they can be either limiting or supporting you. Many of these aspects are combined in the so-called 'onion model.' The model forms the basis for the theory on core reflection, which is the main theory on which this book is based. Several activities in this chapter will help you apply the core reflection approach and support you in getting to know yourself on a deeper level.

Chapter 8 is called *Working with Presence and Mindfulness*. Presence is the experience of being completely in the here-and-now. Mindfulness means being fully aware. These two terms are quite related. You can think a lot about yourself and learn a lot from this book for your professional growth, but ultimately it is important to feel your power 'in the moment' and to be aware of what exactly is happening between you and others in the here-and-now. The central question is: Are you completely present in the moment, with everything that happens, and with full awareness? If you experience presence, it is very supportive to optimal functioning. Great examples of presence are when professional sportsmen, dancers, or Japanese swordfighters are in their best moments. When they are completely present in the moment, they can respond with their full potential to situations that arise.

Chapter 9 is called *Turning Problems into Opportunities for Growth*. In this chapter, we will re-address many of the principles from previous chapters. We will utilize these to deal with everyday problems. Most problems arise from the way we look at a situation and experience it. You will learn how to approach situations differently and how this affects your experience of them, especially in problematic situations. We will help you to deal effectively with limiting thought patterns, images, and feelings, and to rediscover your personal power. Finally, through using these techniques you will learn how problems can become opportunities for growth.

Chapter 10 is called *Working with This Book: Some practical tips*. In this chapter we give advice on how to use this book for both individuals and groups. If you are a coach or teacher who wants to stimulate your group to work from the core, you will find many concrete suggestions and tips in this chapter.

FURTHER EXPLORATION

The View Behind This Book

As you will have seen in the chapter summaries above, this book assumes a broad vision of human potential, a vision in which we don't just look at a person as a thinking being, but in which we also value feelings, needs, and desires. On top of this, we also believe that each person has talents and core qualities which allow for inspiration and effectiveness at work, without ignoring the fact that people can also be exposed to problems. People are very often limited by all sorts of obstacles, and we take this very seriously. We don't at all think that everything will always go smoothly, or that people only have beautiful sides to them, or that you can 'make' every situation into a success. On the other hand, we believe there are many people who can use their inner potential much more strongly, exactly when these problems arise.

This vision is supported by an evolution—or even revolution—in the scientific understanding of psychological growth. Well-known psychologists Seligman and Csikszentmihalyi have influenced the development of a completely new discipline, called *positive psychology*. Seligman, a former president of the American Psychological Association, states that during the last century, psychology has insufficiently acknowledged human potential. Instead, psychologists have become better and better at mapping deficiencies and traumas and finding treatments for them. This is a 'problem-focused' vision; the focus is on analyzing people's history and overcoming problems. In western society, this has led to a certain way of thinking about growth and development. We tend to dig into our past to find the root of the problems in our lives. We try to understand what has happened in the past that created the problem, which we then hope to find a solution for.

Although there are definite benefits to understanding more about your own background, this certainly does not always lead to a solution to today's problems. Sometimes they even get worse, for example, because you might start to think that something is wrong with you. Just this belief system alone can create serious problems. For example, if you think that you are not suited to a certain career, this belief will soon manifest itself in your behavior and hence the belief will become true. We may call this a 'self-fulfilling prophecy,' because now even the search for a solution becomes a problem in itself. This can lead to unnecessary worrying and a sense of being 'stuck.'

This is why Seligman and Csikszentmihalyi—based on scientific research—say that applying a 'problem-focused' vision is not very effective at all. Very few people become happier through it. Positive psychology has gone a different way—one that focuses more on people's strengths and their positive experiences. Increasingly, this discipline is becoming important, because many positive results have been achieved through its application. There have been other developments pointing in the same direction that positive psychology is now taking. For example, in the second half of the twentieth century the psychologists Rogers and Maslow also focused on people's strengths instead of their weaknesses and thus laid the ground for what became known as 'humanistic psychology.' However, contrary to this latter movement, the real strength of positive psychology is its focus on solid empirical research. Through this research, new and powerful methods have been developed to help people find their strengths.

What we are talking about is the shift from focusing on the negative and the problematic, to focusing more on quality, potential, and possibilities. This does not seem to be very easy in western society. We harbor a collective belief system which dictates that life is not easy, or even that we are not allowed to have an easy life; we believe that we have to work hard in order to deserve happiness. So, the conviction is that life is difficult . . . and, of course, this makes it difficult.

Some people caricature the new vision of personal well-being. They say that in this new vision everything is possible, that you can *make* happiness, as long as you think positively. This is not correct, and this caricature has very little to do with positive psychology. What *is* right is that we can learn to deal with our struggles and misfortunes in a way that is different from what we are used to. We can influence our own well-being, not by digging deeply into our problems and trying to 'solve' them, but by starting from our power and potential. Sometimes problems just cannot be solved, but we can learn to deal with them in a different, more positive way. Through this, we develop resilience, which is the capacity to cope with stress and adversity, and to 'bounce back' to a state of more optimal functioning. This may imply that when things go differently from what was expected, one sees the new opportunities this creates and is able to make the most use of them.

However, the positive side is only half the story. In this book, we will also thoroughly cover the other side: the problems people face in day-to-day struggles. However, for us it is ultimately about connecting the negative and the positive sides: How can you utilize your problems to discover your qualities and end up happier and stronger? A lot is known about this scientifically.

Does this mean that we assume that essentially all people are good? According to some people this conflicts with certain religious beliefs. We want to emphasize that in this book, we never say so and are not even suggesting this. Our position is much more pragmatic: every person has many beautiful qualities and talents and it is a shame if these are not expressed to their full potential, while there is every opportunity for it. That is what we focus on.

Professional Development Through a Book?

Is it possible to focus on professional growth using a book? We believe it is, but a book with only theories or good ideas would not be of much use. That is why we have made this a practical handbook, full of activities and exercises that link back to theory. We highlight the interaction between theory and practice and the ability to reflect on your own experiences. Ideally, these three elements (theory, practice, and reflection) should be completely merged in the process of professional development.

This demands a fruitful attitude towards learning, in which your own experiences and reflections, as well theory, are valued equally. What is just as important is to develop a structure in your learning process. It is especially useful to keep switching between experimenting, reflecting on your experiences, doing activities, reading theory, practicing its application, and so forth.

SCIENTIFIC BACKGROUND

The activities in this book are based on scientific research. In this section, we refer to the most important theories that form the basis for many of the activities.

Positive Psychology and Core Qualities

Traditional psychology used to look much more at weakness and deficiency than at what makes people psychologically strong and healthy (Seligman & Csikszentmihalyi, 2000). Positive psychology emphasizes that people have many qualities. These can often be drawn on and developed much more. Seligman (2003) maintains that strengthening human potential, for which many options exist, is at the core of optimal functioning.

The discipline of positive psychology studies qualities like optimism, courage, trust, hope, honesty, and determination (Peterson & Seligman, 2004; Aspinwall & Staudinger, 2003). Seligman (2002, p. 5) calls these the *character strengths* that help people overcome problems, and that can function as a buffer to mental illnesses. We call these strengths 'core qualities.' Seligman emphasizes that such qualities are at the root of positive experiences for psychologically healthy people. The positive power of core qualities can undo the negative emotions from which people suffer (Fredrickson, 1998, 2001, 2002, 2009; Seligman & Peterson, 2003). Seligman and Peterson (2003, p. 306) highlight this with the statement: "Positive emotion undoes negative emotion."

Flow

Flow is what you may experience when you apply your skills in situations that are challenging. It is the feeling of going with the flow, and losing yourself in what you do. Time seems to stand still and everything seems like it just happens by itself. Flow gives you energy and strength. It is also a moment of deep learning (Csikszentmihalyi, 1990, 1992, 1993). We look at flow as an expression of your core; a powerful expression in which your qualities come to the fore. Because of this, flow is an important driver for both professional and personal development. We will go into more detail on flow in the scientific background section of Chapter 5.

Inspiration

Inspiration is also an important term in this book. Inspiration is a living, often energetic, and rich experience in which you feel that you can rise above everyday possibilities (Thrash, Elliot, Maruskin, & Cassidy, 2010a). When you are inspired, you can experience more than usual motivation and deeper insights (a phenomenon also called transcendence), which can give you much clarity and power (Thrash & Elliot, 2003, 2004). When you are inspired, you are also more creative and you work more effortlessly and efficiently than normal (Thrash *et al.*, 2010a, p. 482). Inspiration increases your well-being and gives you a strong feeling of direction and gratefulness (Thrash, Maruskin, Cassidy, Fryer, & Ryan, 2010b). It is clear that inspiration can give a direction to your work and private life that comes directly from who you are and what you want, at your core.

The Broaden-and-Build Model

In this book we emphasize the importance of positive emotions, and we want to help you to find and increase them. This focus is partly based on research into the functions of positive emotions, which has led to the *broaden-and-build model* (Fredrickson, 2001). The basic assumption of this model is that positive emotions increase people's power, broaden their perception, and build important psychological buffers (Garland et al., 2010; Tugade & Fredrickson, 2004). Negative emotions are also necessary for personal growth. However, in general they limit one's strength, perception, and ability to adapt. Fredrickson (2001) and Fredrickson and Losada (2005) hypothesize that positive emotions undo the limiting effects of negative emotions, but there is discussion among researchers about the most beneficial positivity-to-negativity ratio (Brown, Sokal, & Friedman, 2013; Fredrickson, 2013).

The Core and Self-actualization

In this book we often refer to the term 'core,' for example in the title of this chapter. Even though everyone has an image and feeling of their 'core,' this term is difficult to capture in scientific terms. The core is the essence of the feeling that you are who you are. More specifically, it is the integrated experience of being, which is activated when you are completely present to who you are (Riva, Waterworth, Waterworth, & Mantovani, 2009) and utilize your full potential for your own well-being and that of others. The latter is called 'self-actualization' (Hodgins & Knee, 2002).

Being aware of an authentic core inside you is important to be able to function optimally and to fully experience well-being and health (e.g. Tsaousis, Nikolaou, Serdaris, & Judge, 2007). Experiences like 'being true to yourself' and 'autonomy' (Deci & Ryan, 2002) are expressions of the core. Also, the feeling of authenticity—being 'who you really are'—refers to a core in people (Peterson & Seligman, 2004). Almaas (1986, 1998) states that the essence of people is like a multi-faceted diamond, reflecting many qualities. The core is also considered to be the timeless essence of yourself when you experience flow (Csikszentmihalyi, 1992, 1993; see also Chapter 5).

All these different descriptions point to a presence in people, which in this book we refer to as 'the core.' Although western psychology still struggles to define this term, there are many texts in eastern traditions about the core in people, often referred to as 'the Self.' For example, the *Bhagavad Gita*, the sacred book of the Hindus, says: "Some have experienced the Self, in all its perfection; others can talk about it as miraculous. But there are many who don't understand, even when they are listening." It is also interesting that there are cultures, such as Native American cultures, that do not have a term for 'self,' as they experience the self as part of a bigger whole.

Practice, Theory, and Reflection

This book is not only based on a psychological knowledge base, but also on a knowledge base of professional development. Much is known about the relationship between theory and practice in the process of professional growth. For example, it is a common but hardly effective habit to present students in educational programs with a theory in the hope that they will apply this to their professional work. This would seem a logical approach—much useful knowledge is available, so what would make more sense than to present this knowledge to novices so that they can use it in the future? Research has, however, shown that the application of this knowledge is meager. This is called the "transfer problem" (Gegenfurtner, Veermans, Festner, & Gruber, 2009).

This comes with a set of consequences for a book like this one. If this book were to present a lot of knowledge, this might seem fantastic, but it would have very little effect if it was not connected to real personal and practical experiences from the start. Knowledge that is connected to personal experiences is called *situated knowledge* (Brown, Collins, & Duguid, 1989). Through this book we want to develop such 'situated knowledge,' and therefore we will follow—as indicated earlier—an approach that merges practice, reflection, and theory. We will always start with the images and themes you bring through your own experience. We will prompt you in reflection on these images, themes, and experiences, and we will gradually add small pieces of theory to this, while stimulating the translation of this theory to concrete professional behavior. In this way, we follow a pedagogical model called the *theory on levels in learning*, which is much more effective at achieving transfer of knowledge to practice. (For further reading on this, we refer to Korthagen, Kessels, Koster, Lagerwerf, & Wubbels, 2001.)

In the theory of levels in learning, reflection is central for deepening learning processes. This concurs with research by Van Woerkom (2003), which showed that reflection is the key factor in professional development. Van Woerkom found that the strongest professionals often reflect on their own experiences, with the intention of benefiting from them in future situations. However, not all types of reflection are equally beneficial. Mansvelder-Longayroux, Beijaard, and Verloop (2007) and Hoekstra (2007) showed that an important distinction can be made between *behavior-oriented* and *meaning-oriented reflection*. The first type of reflection is aimed at the question 'What should I do?', whereas the second is aimed more at finding the meaning of the situation and assessing what is or was essential about it. Research has shown that meaning-oriented reflection is more important to professional development than behavior-oriented reflection, which generally focuses only on the short-term. This is why we aim to stimulate meaning-oriented reflection in this book.

Two factors that also increase transfer are *interaction* and *cooperation* (Korthagen *et al.*, 2001; Milanese, Iani, & Rubichi, 2010). This is why the activities in this book are often aimed at working with others. Finally, transfer is stronger when working from a positive perspective (Brand, Reimer, & Opwis, 2007). Hence, our emphasis is on letting go of limitations, and drawing on positive expectations, ideals, core qualities, and personal inspiration. But ultimately, the most important thing is for the person to be motivated to apply what they have learned from experience using their own willpower (Gegenfurtner *et al.*, 2009).

Each time we describe the pedagogical principles, we will also indicate how they should be applied in educational situations. Ideally, teachers or coaches work with this same pedagogical vision when developing the knowledge and skills of their students or mentees. Central to this is to start with the personal experience and questions or concerns arising from the participants in the learning process, while stimulating meaning-oriented reflection and interaction between participants. We will elaborate on the question of how to use this book in groups and other educational situations in Chapter 10, where we will also further explore the pedagogical vision behind this book.

2 Tapping into the Power of Your Core Qualities

Many people will still remember that one special teacher they once had. Whenever you were in their classroom something special would happen. Everyone would be excitedly listening to what was being said. This teacher would not only have a great amount of knowledge and be able to explain things really well, but would be especially enthusiastic and inspiring. It was the special combination of competencies and authentic personality which made all the difference. As a student you would be looking forward to this teacher's lessons. You would learn things that you would remember for the rest of your life.

What are Core Qualities?

What makes people excel at their work? This seems to depend quite a lot on the profession. For example, a teacher has to do completely different things from a nurse or engineer. The engineer has to master a variety of technical skills, but also has to have strong interpersonal skills in order to relate well with his co-workers. Every profession requires its own set of skills. Lists exist for these skills; we call them competency lists. However, the way that someone applies these competences strongly depends on their personality. This is true for all professions.

If someone is very motivated to perform a certain task really well, in whatever profession, you will notice this in their actions. They concentrate, know what they want, and do not want to deliver a mediocre product. In this case, they are using a set of personal qualities: motivation, the ability to concentrate, focus, and ambition. We call these types of qualities in a person *core qualities* (Ofman, 2000). They determine the quality of someone's work.

If, for example, a person's strength lies in cooperation, he or she will perform better in a team than working individually. If someone is good at creating visions and working from intuitive insights, this person is often better at developing new plans than at doing work that requires more attention to detail. Only if, within their profession, there is enough space to use their own unique qualities can this person be inspired to work and learn effectively. This requires knowing your own strengths, qualities, talents, and ideals so that you can develop yourself according to who you really are.

It is not without reason that employers often ask at a job interview what your strengths are, because it makes you a strong professional if you know your own core qualities and use them effectively. This chapter focuses on supporting you in this.

2   Introductory Activity: Looking at What Makes People Special

Each person is unique and uses specific qualities. By recognizing these qualities in people, what makes them special also becomes clearer. You can learn to recognize core qualities in people by looking at what makes them special and strong in their work.

Introductory Activity: Looking at What Makes People Special		
Goal: Recognizing and naming core qualities. **Materials**: None.	1-1 2-1 3-1	Think of a person you find special (e.g. an inspiring teacher, creative neighbor, caring family member, etc.) Choose a few aspects of this person that make him or her special to you. **Write down:** This person is . . . This person is . . . This person is . . . These types of character traits are also called *core qualities*. **Write down:** • What is the effect on you when the person you chose uses these core qualities? What do you experience? • What is the effect of each of these core qualities on: (a) the person? (b) his/her environment?

Examples of core qualities are creativity, curiosity, justice, precision, openness, persistence, enthusiasm, and courage. Other core qualities that may be characteristic for a person are love, care, sensitivity, and humor. The great thing is that most core qualities have a wide application. For example, the core quality of commitment can be used in many situations; you can use persistence in many areas to achieve your goals. The term core quality has been chosen because such a quality is unique about that person, something that has to do with their core. Every person has many qualities 'in their core.' We show this in Figure 2.1 in which the core of a person is pictured like a multi-faceted diamond.

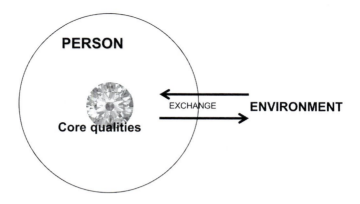

Figure 2.1   Core qualities belonging to the 'diamond within'

3   Introductory Activity: Recognizing Your Own Core Qualities

The image of the diamond perfectly suits the new term that has been introduced recently in psychology: *psychological capital*. You could say that your psychological capital is stored inside your core, in your core qualities. There exists the capability to use your strengths in your life and, hence, also at work. The arrow in Figure 2.1 indicates that with your core qualities you have an important influence on your environment, because when you use these core qualities, people around you will notice this. It also works the other way around, for influences from your environment affect you and stimulate you to use your core qualities.

Perhaps you do not even notice this anymore because you take your core qualities for granted. However, it is important to recognize them, to feel them, and to use them consciously in order to achieve your maximum potential.

Introductory Activity: Recognizing Your Own Core Qualities		
Goal: Recognizing your own core qualities and considering their possible applications. **Materials**: None.	1-1	Choose a situation from your work, study, or home in which you experienced a success, for example, something you are proud of.
	2-1	**Write down:** • Which core qualities did you use in this situation? • In which other situations do you use these core qualities as well? • What is the effect of this on you and what effect does it have on others in your environment?
	3-1	In which other situations and places could you also use these core qualities?

FURTHER EXPLORATION

The term core quality is an alternative to the term *character strengths*, which is a central notion in a new branch of psychology called positive psychology. In 2000, Seligman, who was then president of the American Psychological Association, and Csikszentmihalyi, who is known for his publications on flow, co-presented a new vision in psychology. They stated that during the second part of the previous century, psychology had taken a wrong direction. According to them, psychologists have focused too much on the traumas and deficiencies of people (Seligman & Csikszentmihalyi, 2000). Famous is their statement: "Treatment is not just fixing what is broken: it is nurturing what is best" (p. 4). According to Seligman and Csikszentmihalyi it is important to focus on the strengths of people, as a way of promoting their well-being.

Positive psychology has by now become a successful branch of psychology within which much interesting empirical research has been done. This research has shown new and powerful opportunities for people to find their own strengths. It has also been shown that this leads to higher levels of happiness.

4 Recognizing Core Qualities in Situations

Quickly and easily recognizing and experiencing core qualities is an important skill. After all, the moment you recognize your own and others' core qualities, you can use them more deliberately. Having the awareness of others' core qualities can activate your own. For example, when you work with someone who shows much care for other people, this may stimulate your own sense of care. The more you try to tap into the power of your own core qualities, the more this helps you improve your own actions and cooperation with others.

In this activity, you will discover core qualities in pictures of people. This way you can easily learn to quickly and smoothly recognize and name core qualities in people in all kinds of situations.

Recognizing Core Qualities in Situations		
Goal: Recognizing core qualities in pictures and learning to use them more effectively. **Materials:** Core qualities pictures (see @, pdf #1).	1-1	Choose six photos from the pile of core qualities pictures. **Write down for each:** • Which core qualities can you see? How do you recognize these? • What is the positive effect of each of these core qualities?

2-2	Exchange with a partner. Which core qualities can you see, how do you recognize these, and what is the positive effect of each of these core qualities? In your pair, do you see the same core qualities in the pictures? Why do you think this is so, or why not?
3-G	Discuss with the whole group: How can you recognize core qualities? What is the power of core qualities and how can you see this?
4-1	Now choose a few situations in the coming week in which you are going to notice the core qualities of people or students you work with and write these down. **Write down:** • Which situations did you choose? • How are you going to notice the core qualities and how will you describe them?
5-G	Discuss briefly and make appointments to follow up, in order to discuss the core qualities you saw and how you recognized them in the situations.

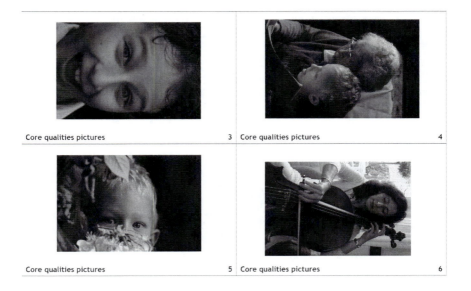

Core qualities pictures 3	Core qualities pictures 4
Core qualities pictures 5	Core qualities pictures 6

Examples of 'Core qualities pictures' cards

The theory of positive psychology states that people have the potential to use and develop their core qualities. The thing that is different for each person, however, is which qualities they are used to applying and the way in which they do this. These differences can be the result of 'nature or nurture.' These differences will never completely disappear, but that is not what is important. The point is that it is possible to learn and apply a broader range of qualities than you are used to, and this will increase your power. You can always develop core qualities, even the ones you have hardly used until now.

5 Recognizing Different Types of Core Qualities

In the next activity, you will compare and rank different core qualities, which will help you to learn more about them and the differences between them. You will also learn more about the effect they can have.

Recognizing Different Types of Core Qualities		
Goal: Observing the differences between core qualities and naming these. **Materials:** Core qualities cards (@, pdf #6) and some blank cards.	1-1	Put all the cards with core qualities in front of you. Split them into three different groups: • a group with the quality of thinking • a group with the quality of feeling • a group with the quality of wanting. If you are in doubt about the place of a card in one of these groups, put it aside. You can also write down more qualities on the blank cards and add them to the groups. **Write down:** According to you, which core qualities belong to which group?
	2-2	Discuss: • Which core qualities did you place in which group and why? • What is the difference among the groups? • Which cards did you leave out? Why?
	3-G	Exchange. Focus on the core qualities of thinking, feeling, and wanting. Are there also combinations of these? (see Figure 2.2; @ pdf #15)

4-1	Choose from each group one core quality you know well, either from yourself or someone else. This gives you three core qualities. **Write down:** What do you think the person and their environment get out of using each of these core qualities?
5-2	Discuss your answers. Discuss what you get out of using these core qualities.
6-G	Exchange and discuss the characteristics you found.
7-1	Now choose for each group a core quality you do not apply much, but which could be useful to you. **Write down:** • Which one did you choose? • How could it be useful for you (e.g. in which situations)? • How can you start to use this core quality effectively?
7-G	Briefly discuss your chosen core qualities and how to improve your application of these.

Creativity	Patience
Core qualities 1	Core qualities 2
Initiative	Precision
Core qualities 3	Core qualities 4

Examples of 'Core qualities' cards

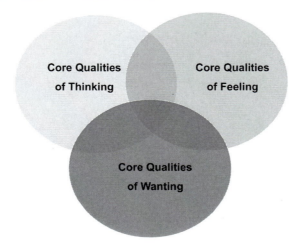

Figure 2.2   Three types of core qualities

In the activity above, you may have discovered that the three groups of core qualities somehow overlap (as shown in Figure 2.2).

6   Increasing Your Skills by Applying Core Qualities

Core qualities and professional skills complement each other. For effective professional behavior, both core qualities and skills are important. For example, you can exercise your skills to tell a story to children, but the way in which you tell the story is decided by certain qualities like imagination, empathy, contact, or social intelligence. In other words, a skill is 'colored' and gets a certain strength through the application of core qualities. For learning, too, both core qualities and skills are necessary. In order to study successfully, you need the skill to read a book, but also enthusiasm for the subject and willpower to continue. To state it more precisely: ultimately it is all about *integrating skills and core qualities*.

It seems that you learn a skill better and with more joy if you consciously apply and use the appropriate core qualities. This is the reason that in this activity we will look at the combination of skills and core qualities. You will take some skills which are necessary for your work or studies, and for each skill look at the core qualities that are especially relevant. You will also explore the value of really applying the skills in connection with these core qualities. You can, of course, also reflect on the question of how you can improve your use of certain core qualities in relation to professional skills.

Increasing Your Skills by Applying Core Qualities

Goal: For each skill, recognizing and naming the most relevant core qualities.

Materials: If possible, a list of skills relevant for your profession/ education, and possibly 'Core qualities' cards (@, pdf #6).

1-1 Choose three skills that are relevant for your education or your profession.
Write down for each skill:
• Which core qualities do you think go with this skill?
• How do you recognize if you apply these core qualities with the skill?

2-2 Compare your findings in pairs. What are the similarities and differences?

3-G Exchange within the group. Which core qualities go with which skill? Does the application of these qualities make a difference?

4-4 Form groups of four and exchange your findings. Focus on the question: What is the role of core qualities in (these) skills? What happens when you consciously apply these core qualities when using the skills?
Formulate as a group:
• A statement about the connection between skills and core qualities
• A statement about how you can optimally profit from the core qualities for the skills you discussed.

5-G Exchange in the whole group. What is the benefit of combining core qualities and skills?

6-1 Choose one of the core qualities you described in 4-4 to apply in your work/education during the coming week.
Write down:
• Which core quality did you choose and why this one?
• When and how will you try to apply it in the coming week?
• How will you decide if this works?

7 Expanding Your Core Qualities

Which core qualities do you use often, what does this say about your character, and what is the effect of these core qualities? To explore this, in the next activity you will select qualities that you recognize in yourself from the cards. You will also think about the question of how to apply these qualities more or how to expand on them by also using other qualities.

Expanding Your Core Qualities		
Goal: Comparing core qualities and recognizing them inside yourself. **Materials:** 'Core qualities' cards (@, pdf #6) and some blank cards.	1-1	Choose from the series of cards the qualities you find really suit you. Put these in front of you. If there are any missing qualities that you have, write these down on blank cards. **Write down:** • How important is each of these core qualities for you? • What does each of these core qualities say about who you are?
	2-2	Compare each other's cards and explain how and when you use these qualities.
	3-G	Brief exchange. Focus in the discussion on how you recognize your core qualities and the positive effect of using them.
	4-1	Choose from your cards the three core qualities you think you apply the most. **Write down:** • When do you especially apply these qualities? • What is the positive effect for you and others of applying these core qualities? • How can you make best use of these qualities in your profession?
	5-2	Compare your results. • Do you recognize these core qualities in each other? • What is the positive effect of these? • How can you make best use of these qualities in your profession?
	6-G	Brief exchange.
	7-1	In the coming weeks, focus especially on using the positive effects of your core qualities. Look for situations in which you can apply them consciously. **Write down:** • When and how will you try to apply your core qualities? • Which positive outcome do you want to achieve? • How will you determine afterwards whether you achieved this outcome?

8   Applying New Core Qualities

Imagine that you are very creative, enthusiastic, and have a lot of energy. This can sometimes make you seem impatient to others. Your behavior is determined by this energy and a certain impatience. In this example, you will learn to apply the core qualities of peace, relaxation, and the quality of seeing things in perspective to create a strong balance. You would become an enthusiastic and creative person who also radiates a certain calmness. If you start to apply new core qualities consistently for a long period of time, they will become part of your personality, and in this way you will develop.

In the next activity, you will select from the core quality cards those that you barely or never apply, but which could possibly have a positive effect on you. Finally, you will choose two core qualities to focus on applying consciously in the coming weeks.

Applying New Core Qualities

Goal: Observing the core qualities you hardly or never apply, and choosing two that could benefit you.

Materials:
'Core qualities' cards (@, pdf #6) and some blank cards.

1-1	Choose from the series of cards those core qualities that you hardly or never apply. Put these next to each other in front of you. If there are any missing qualities you would like to add, write them on blank cards. **Write down:** • Which core qualities do you not apply much? • What does this say about you?
2-2	Compare your results with your partner. Do you recognize this in each other?
3-G	Brief exchange. Focus on how you can benefit from expanding your core qualities.
4-1	Now choose two core qualities from this selection which are possibly beneficial to you. **Write down:** • Which core qualities did you choose and why? • Give some examples of positive outcomes from applying these core qualities. • What effect could it have on others when you start to apply these qualities?
5-2	Compare your results. What are the benefits to your environment when you apply these core qualities?
6-G	Brief exchange.
7-1	**Write down:** • How can you make better use of these core qualities? • What is your intention for the coming weeks?

	8-2	Compare your findings. Help each other to make the intentions more concrete.
	9-G	Brief exchange and listing of tips on how you can start to apply these core qualities concretely and how you can promote a positive outcome.

9 Increasing Your Energy by Applying Your Core Qualities in the Here-And-Now

Applying your core qualities gives you energy. It is important to know how to do this effectively and easily. The following activity helps you to apply your core qualities.

Increasing Your Energy by Applying Your Core Qualities in the Here-And-Now		
Goal: Applying your core qualities in your current activities. Learning to give core feedback. **Materials:** Blank cards and possibly 'Core qualities' cards (@, pdf #6).	1-1	Which core quality helps you to have more energy in the here-and-now and enjoy what you are doing more? **Write down:** • What is this core quality? • How does this make you feel right now? Write this core quality on a card and put it in front of you. Apply the core quality consciously during this activity.
	2-2	Exchange the reasons for choosing these core qualities. Practice in your conversation how to apply these core qualities.
	3-G	Exchange. Everyone puts the card in front of them and focuses on applying it in the here-and-now.
	4-1	Spend a few minutes of applying this core quality. **Write down:** • How is it going? • What do you get from applying the core quality? • How can you make sure you really do it? • Do you start to see the need for another core quality as well? If so, which? • Apply this one now!
	5-2	Exchange.
	6-G	Exchange.

10   Working with the Core Qualities that Give Meaning to Your Life

The ancient Greeks like Plato and Aristotle talked about certain core qualities they found extremely important because they form the basis for a healthy society. These qualities are also called *virtues*. They give meaning to life and have a positive effect on civilization as a whole. Some virtues often mentioned are wisdom, humanity, and justice. The next activity will help you to get more clarity regarding those values that give you more direction in your life.

Working with the Core Qualities that Give Meaning to Your Life

Goal: Comparing and experiencing the core qualities in your life and compiling a personal core value profile.

Materials: 'Core qualities' cards (@, pdf #6) and some blank cards.

1-1	Take the core qualities cards and arrange them so that they form a wall, pillar, or pyramid. At the bottom, place the cards you find most important. This is the foundation. At the top, place the cards that you find less important. Qualities you don't apply or find irrelevant you can put aside. If there are any qualities missing, you can write them on blank cards and add them to the structure.	
2-2	Exchange and help each other to perfect the structure.	
3-G	Share: What are important core values of the participants?	
4-1	Take a piece of paper and write or draw your wall, pillar, or pyramid. **Write down:** • Which core qualities form your foundation? • Why these, and what does this say about your values in work and life in general? • If there was one new core quality you would like to add to the foundation, one that would really be valuable for you, which one would that be? • What would applying this one bring you?	
5-2	Exchange.	
6-G	Discuss in the whole group: • How are core qualities and values connected? • Which strategies can you apply to develop certain core qualities further?	
7-1	**Write down:** • Which core quality did you add to your foundation, and why is this quality important to you? • What are you going to do concretely to apply this core quality in the coming weeks (where it is appropriate and positive for you and others)?	

29

11 Applying Your Core Qualities Specifically

Core qualities are present inside you from the moment you are born, but you can keep developing them. The best way to develop your core qualities is by *doing*: applying them often and in a focused manner. If you are aware of a core quality and apply it consciously, while noting the positive outcome of this, you will strengthen this quality inside yourself. However, you have to use your *will* in this: you have to be prepared to do so in a focused and systematic manner.

The next activity can help you with this. This activity will be most interesting if you link it to something you feel less confident about, for example to a situation in which you could apply more patience, trust, precision, or a broader perspective.

Applying Your Core Qualities Specifically		
Goal: Applying a core quality in a concrete task. Look during and after the situation at what this has added. **Materials:** Blank cards, 'Core qualities in action' cards (@, pdf #7).	1-1	You will start to work on a task (something you choose yourself or one that has to be done). Before you start, think about which core quality will help you to enjoy the task more and perform it better. **Write down:** • Which task did you choose? • Which core quality will you apply to make this task easier and more enjoyable? • What can this core quality give you? • How do you want to apply this core quality? How will you do this exactly?
	2-2	Exchange. • Which core quality did you choose? • How will you apply it? • What will you get from that?
	3-G	Discussion in the whole group. Focus on what a core quality can give you.
	4-1	Start your task and apply the core quality. At three moments, evaluate how things are going. For example, use a watch to time a moment of reflection at one-third through, two-thirds through, and at the end of the task.
	5-1	At one-third: How is it going? Are you really applying the core quality? **Write down:** • If it works, how are you applying the core quality? • If it does not work, what is going wrong? Is it really this core quality you need to apply or do you feel that you might need another? • What helps you to apply the core quality?

6-2	Exchange how you applied the core quality and how that went.
7-G	Discussion in the group.
8-1	At two-thirds, repeat step 5-1, and at the end of your task, repeat step 6-2 and 7-G.
9-4	Exchange your experiences.
10-G	Gather insights.

Structuredness	Humor
Can be seen in:	Can be seen in:
....	....
....	....
....	....
....	....
....	....
....	....
Core qualities in action 1	Core qualities in action 2
Social intelligence	**Enthusiasm**
Can be seen in:	Can be seen in:
....	....
....	....
....	....
....	....
....	....
Core qualities in action 3	Core qualities in action 4

Examples of 'Core qualities in action' cards

12   Applying Core Qualities in Difficult Situations

We often experience situations as being tricky or difficult if we cannot apply the right core qualities. For example, you are nervous because you do not think that you are able to do something well. The result can be that because of this tension, you will do it even less well. You get frustrated, tired, and really want to stop. In this case you could, for example, apply the core quality of 'sense of perspective' and assume that it doesn't have to be perfect, or that you try your best and let it go the way it will (it will be what it will be). Part of your stress can dissolve through this. Another option is to apply a little more precision, through which you will concentrate on what is really important. You could also apply humor and have more fun at what you are doing, and through that humor you may gain more energy. Using core qualities this way makes a real difference. Unfortunately, people will often do the opposite in difficult situations; they will look at what is going wrong and put extra pressure on themselves, and in this way limit their potential (Brand *et al.*, 2007).

The next activity is a preparation for a situation in which you have to do something you struggle with. You will look for a core quality that can help you.

Applying Core Qualities in Difficult Situations		
Goal: Applying core qualities in one of your activities. Learning to name the core qualities. **Materials:** Possibly the 'Core qualities' cards (@, pdf #6).	1-1	Choose a conversation you are scheduled to have soon, or choose a certain type of professional relationship you want to strengthen. Which quality helps you to feel more energy and perform the chosen activity with more joy? Can you feel this core quality inside yourself? **Write down:** • Which core quality is it? • How does this core quality feel to you? What energy do you get from it? Put a card with that core quality in front of you.
	2-2	Exchange why you wrote down this core quality. Practice here and now with applying the chosen core qualities.
	3-G	Discussion in the whole group. Everyone puts the card with the core quality in front of them, and in the conversation everyone will focus on applying this one core quality.
	4-1	Spend a few minutes applying this core quality. **Write down:** • How is it going? • What do you get from applying this core quality? • How can you make sure that you will really do this and keep doing it? • Do you notice that you need another core quality as well? If so, which? Apply this one now!
	5-2	Exchange in pairs.
	6-G	Discussion in the group.

13   Balancing Core Qualities

People often mention their core qualities in the same sentence as they mention their 'weaknesses'. They will for example say: "Yes, enthusiasm is my core quality, but it is really also my downfall!"; thus they turn the positive quality into something negative. We believe that enthusiasm is a fantastic core quality and it could be useful for that person to develop another core quality some more, such as sensitivity for the environment or his or her own boundaries. In this way, the quality of enthusiasm does not need to be considered negative. It is all about the right balance between core qualities, a balance which leads to optimal functioning in a certain situation or context.

Balancing Core Qualities		
Goal: Finding a balance in applying core qualities. **Materials:** 'Core qualities' cards (@, pdf #6) and some blank cards.	1-1	Take the core qualities cards and choose the core qualities that really suit you. On the blank cards write some additional ones. **Write down:** • Which core quality did you choose? • What is the benefit of this quality to you and your environment?
	2-2	Exchange. • Which core qualities do you have? • What are the benefits of these?
	3-G	Brief exchange in the group. Now link your reflections to balancing the core qualities.
	4-1	See if you can place an opposite core quality against each of your qualities chosen at step 1-1. For example, enthusiasm with inner peace, flexibility with persistence. **Write down:** • Which core qualities did you place together? • What is the positive effect on you and your environment if you can apply these two core qualities at the same time?
	5-2	Exchange. • What links did you make between the core qualities? • What is the positive effect of applying these simultaneously?

6-G	Exchange with a focus on how to practice this in a real situation.	
7-1	**Write down:** • Which pair of core qualities is positive for you and how are you going to apply them together in the near future? • How are you going to determine the positive effect on this for you and your environment?	

14 Recognizing and Naming Core Qualities in a Conversation

People find it important to be seen and recognized for who they are. This is why conversations are much more successful if you recognize each other's core qualities and name them. For example, you could say: "I find you very creative," "I enjoy your honesty," or "You are such a decisive person!". Of course, this has to be authentic. In such interactions people often open up and communication can be deepened.

In the next activity, you practice a conversation with someone else in which you name the core qualities you see in the person while you are talking. This is an important exercise which helps you to start to do this more often in work situations. Most people need to get over a barrier before they have the courage to do this, and this activity will help you in this. Perhaps you will also discover what this activity brings you or the other person, and this can stimulate you to name the core qualities more often in others.

Recognizing and Naming Core Qualities in a Conversation		
Goal: Practicing giving feedback on core qualities you observe in others. **Materials:** None.	1-1	Choose an experience of success at work or a personal ideal.
	2-2	Tell each other about this success/ideal while the other is listening (2 × 3 minutes). As a listener you should pay attention to the core qualities you observe in the other person (e.g. enthusiasm, commitment, courage, decisiveness, willpower, passion, etc.). The moment you recognize a core quality in the other person you name it (so do not wait until the end of the three minutes). If you find it difficult to recognize a core quality, one suggestion is to look at what happens with you through the other person's energy. This will make it easier to name the quality in the other person which causes this experience in you. At the end of the discussion, write down which core qualities you named in the other person, and give the list to them.

3-G	Have a group discussion with the focus on: • How do you recognize core qualities during a conversation? • How do you give feedback on core qualities? • How does it feel to receive this feedback? • What is the difference between feedback on someone's core qualities and feedback on what someone does well?
4-1	**Write down:** • How can you help yourself to recognize core qualities in a conversation quickly and easily? • Which of your own core qualities can help you with this?
5-2	Form new pairs and have another conversation as in 2-2 (again 2 × 3 minutes). Give each other feedback on core qualities during the conversation and again make a list of the qualities you named.
6-G	Discuss in the group: • Is it becoming easier? • What helps you in becoming good at this?
7-1	**Write down:** How will you practice recognizing and naming the core qualities in others?

15   Recognizing Core Qualities of a Group

Just as each person has core qualities, so do groups, teams, or organizations. The following activity will help you to look at the core qualities of a team or group. You explore the core qualities that come out strongly and others that in your opinion deserve more attention.

Recognizing Core Qualities of a Group		
Goal: Recognizing the core qualities of a group. Determining those core qualities that increase the opportunities of that group.	1-1	Look at the group of which you are a member. Name three core qualities that you see as a strength of this group. **Write down:** • What are the three core qualities that stand out to you? • How can you see that? Would others say the same about this group? Explain why.
Materials: Materials to make a core quality poster of the group.	2-2	Compare the chosen core qualities and discuss. Try to justify your opinion.

3-4	Compare in the team of four how your core qualities are different and try to find a common denominator.
4-G	Discussion in the whole group.
5-1	Which core qualities can you use to make the group stronger? **Write down:** • Which core qualities are they according to you? • Why those? What would change in the group when you apply them? • What can you do concretely to use these core qualities more?
6-4	Compare and try to list the core qualities that help the group to function better.
7-G	Discussion in the group. Collect the suggestions.
8-4	How can you help each other to apply these core qualities?
9-G	Make a poster with the core qualities that are there and those that are going to be worked on. Try to make it look nice (see Chapter 10 for poster suggestions).

SCIENTIFIC BACKGROUND

Characteristics of Core Qualities

The term *core qualities* is used in this book to describe personal characteristics that have a positive effect on people's lives. Every person has these qualities, which, if developed and applied appropriately, protect against problems and help to build, strengthen, and maintain a healthy mental condition (Seligman, 2003; Peterson & Seligman, 2004). Core qualities are positive personal mechanisms that invoke satisfaction, which doesn't just benefit the person, but also benefits their environment.

Seligman (2003) and Peterson and Seligman (2004) list the following characteristics of core qualities (which they call *character strengths*):

1. A core quality adds to the 'good life' of the person and others. Although core qualities determine how someone deals with resistance, the focus is on the feeling of fulfillment.
2. Although a core quality can bring about a certain desired result, such as the experience of well-being, competence, health, satisfaction at

work, etc., each core quality in itself has a positive value, separate of any outcome. The expression of a core quality by someone never takes away from other people around them.

3. A core quality manifests itself in the functioning of a person (their thoughts, feelings, and/or actions) in such a way that it can be experienced by others. A core quality is a characteristic of a person in the sense that there is a possibility of generalizing between situations and stability over time.

4. A core quality is expressed through stories, myths, legends, symbols, etc.

5. There are children who show a certain core quality very strongly from an extremely young age. This is not the case for all core qualities.

6. There are people in whom one core quality is completely absent.

7. Society has institutions and rituals which focus on cultivating core qualities and keeping their application alive.

Seligman and Peterson (2003, p. 309) emphasize that an important result of drawing on a core quality is the experience of fulfillment. This experience of fulfillment also has a positive influence on the person's environment. Aside from experiencing fulfillment, another important characteristic of core qualities is that they are expressions of important core values or virtues (Seligman & Peterson, 2003). According to Sheldon and Kasser (2001, p. 43) they are closely connected to the fulfillment of basic psychological needs (see Chapter 4) and *self-actualization* (Kasser, 2002).

In their handbook *Character strengths and virtues,* Peterson and Seligman (2004) offer a scientific discussion of the core qualities of people. They state that all people have core qualities, in other words, they are innate. However, outside influences and life experiences can cause some core qualities to become more developed and others to slide into the background. The more you apply and develop your core qualities in your interaction with the world, the happier and better functioning you will be.

Peterson and Seligman (2004) make a distinction between three types of core qualities:

1. Core qualities that you apply spontaneously in a specific situation;

2. Core qualities that you apply often as an expression of your character;

3. Essential core qualities that are seen as virtues or core values.

The last is at the basis of a healthy society. In this context, Dahlsgaard, Peterson, and Seligman (2005) mention the qualities of wisdom, courage, humanity, justice, patience, and transcendence.

In positive psychology, the core qualities of people are seen as their psychological capital (Luthans, Youssef, & Avolio, 2007), which helps to develop *resilience* (Enthoven, 2007; Masten & Reed, 2002). Resilience is the capacity to keep functioning well under difficult circumstances. This implies not being put down by disappointments, but instead seeing new opportunities through them and giving them shape (Friborg, Hjemdal, Martinussen, & Rosenvinge, 2009).

Core Qualities in the Classroom

Ruit and Korthagen (2013) explored the impact of stimulating young students in the Netherlands (ages 7–12-years-old) to consciously use their personal qualities. Based on a similar experiment carried out with adults (Seligman, Steen, Park, & Peterson, 2005), these students were asked to use one core quality (identified with a questionnaire) each day for one week, and use it again in a different way. The research question was: What are the effects of this relatively simple intervention? Apparently, students were capable of recognizing their own core qualities and in linking these with their actions after a relatively short intervention by their teachers. Through this study, it became clear that it is possible to influence the personal growth of children through a short and simple intervention by building on their core qualities. This research opens up completely new ways of thinking about teaching and learning in schools.

3 Using Three Information Channels

Thinking, Feeling, and Wanting

> Imagine a school principal who is very good at creating new methods
> of instruction at his school and at solving financial and practical prob-
> lems. However, he is not so good when it comes to emotions. He never
> asks how others are doing, how they are feeling, and what occupies
> them. His teachers and students find him very competent, but they
> miss the feeling of 'warmth.'

In the previous chapter, we saw that people have many different core qualities. Core qualities such as precision, analytical skills, and discernment all
emphasize thinking. There are other core qualities that have more to do
with feeling. Examples of these are care and compassion, both of which are
important in interactions with students and colleagues.

16 Orientation Activity: Experiencing the Difference between Thinking and Feeling

Thinking and feeling are two different 'channels' that are used by people who
work in education. You can observe this in many different situations. In education, which involves a high level of interaction with other people, it is important to think properly about content, goals, and strategies. But it is also necessary
to really connect with others. This connection is not something that happens
merely by using one's 'thinking.' Connecting well requires empathy and sensitivity to the other person's experience, and it requires you to express your own
emotions. However, you need to feel these emotions first. This might sound
strange, but it is helpful for optimal professional behavior to feel and experience your emotions. Just look at what happens with your emotions when you
think of your favorite student or colleague. What do you experience when you
see and imagine this person? Do you notice anything in your body, your stomach, your heart, or your breathing? Now imagine your most difficult student
or colleague: What do you feel now? Do you also have a physical reaction to
thinking about this person in your stomach, your heart, or your breathing?

Feelings and experiences are important, but we don't always notice them.
Some people experience and feel their emotions only when these are very

intense. But their milder emotions will also have an unconscious effect on their actions. Are you aware of this? Can you 'feel your feelings'?

Some people say: "I am more of a thinker, and I don't feel much." For such a person, the mind can be their strength, and therefore an important quality of that person. However, someone like this could certainly learn to feel their feelings more and make greater use of their feeling-channel.

Orientation Activity: Experiencing the Difference between Thinking and Feeling

Goal: Getting in touch with 'feeling' and 'thinking,' and experiencing the difference between these two channels.

Materials: None.

1-1 **Write down:**
What do you think is the definition of inspiration? If necessary, you could look this up on the internet or in a dictionary.

2-1 Think of some situations in which you are usually very inspired. Experience this feeling of inspiration. Where do you feel this in your body and how does it affect you? Draw an image or symbol that represents inspiration for you.

3-1 **Write down:**
• What is the difference between (a) thinking analytically about inspiration and (b) experiencing inspiration?
• Which of the two information channels (thinking and feeling) can give you more information when it comes to inspiration?

---

17 Orientation Activity: Using the Information from Thinking, Feeling, and Wanting

Besides feeling and thinking, there is a third important channel: wanting. After all, you will put great effort into something you really want. 'Wanting' includes one's desires and needs. Two examples are your need to express your individuality or your desire to have pleasant relationships at work.

Orientation Activity: Using the Information from Thinking, Feeling, and Wanting

Goal: Exploring the differences and connections between thinking, feeling, and wanting.

1-1 Remember a current or past situation in your work that you found very difficult (or alternatively, very inspiring); for example, an interaction with a class or with an individual student.

Materials: None.

Write down:
- What are your thoughts about this situation?
- How do you feel about the situation? Can you also observe this in your body? If so, where?
- What do you *want* in this situation? What is your *desire*? What do you *need*?

2-1 **Write down:**
- How do you experience the difference between thinking, feeling, and wanting?
- In what way does your thinking, feeling, and wanting influence the situation? And what is the difference between them?

Maybe you already discovered in the previous activity that your thinking, feeling, and wanting each do something different in the situation. You could consider how you can use the information from each of these three 'channels' to improve your connection with others and in particular to be more yourself. What we are aiming at is the skill to use these three types of information in such a way that they complement each other. If you are able to do this, you can make the best use of your potential. We will explain this with a metaphor. Imagine thought being based in the head, feeling in the heart, and wanting in the stomach. You are at your best when you pay equal attention to all these three areas. We use the expression of the 'elevator'; it is important that the elevator runs smoothly up and down past the three levels (head, heart, and stomach); see Figure 3.1.

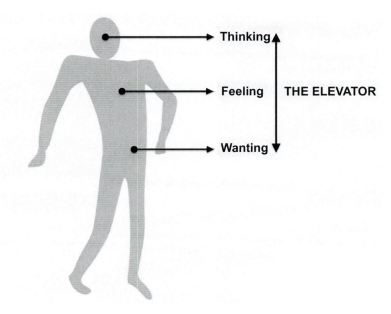

Figure 3.1   The elevator

The three areas of thinking, feeling, and wanting complement each other:

- Thinking allows you to understand, plan, analyze, and discuss.
- Feeling allows you to experience how something affects you. Does it fit with you or not, does it feel good or not, is it right for you or not?
- Wanting gives you information about the direction you want to take. It is the energy that helps you to make your life or work the way you want it to be.

We see thinking, feeling, and wanting at the root of all actions. At work, many people use thinking as the primary basis of what they do. If this is really their only channel, they build on only part of their potential. If you only use the information from one channel, you miss a lot of important information from the other two. Other people become very easily emotional and barely use their mind. Others, again, are solely focused on the wanting: 'I want this to be different!' If you are stuck in thinking about a problem, it can help to bring your attention to your feelings or to ask yourself what you actually want. If you are stuck in your emotions, it can help for you to call on your thoughts, etc. We call it 'using the elevator' when you can effortlessly switch between thinking, feeling, and wanting.

FURTHER EXPLORATION

Figure 3.1 illustrates three important areas that you can think of as people's information channels: thinking, feeling, and wanting. In our culture there has, for a long time, been an overemphasis on the rational mind. Nowadays, people are starting to appreciate that thinking, feeling, and wanting are all important and closely connected. In the rest of this chapter we will have a closer look at the three areas of thinking, feeling, and wanting. We will start with thinking.

18 Becoming Aware of Your Thoughts in a Difficult Situation

When you use your thoughts, you can organize the world into concepts and structures. By doing this you can bring clarity to the things you perceive and experience. When you are thinking you are also selecting: you bring the constant flow of impressions and information back to something you can process with your mind. This is one of the ways of getting a grasp on the world and your life, which makes thinking a powerful tool.

The thought process hardly ever pauses. But restless thinking, for example under pressure, can also lead to stress and weakness. There are, however, several ways to increase the power of your thoughts. This activity will help you to observe how you think in a difficult situation. Is there a way of thinking that would be more useful in this situation?

Becoming Aware of Your Thoughts in a Difficult Situation

Goal: Becoming aware of your thinking and thought patterns, and their effect, in a given situation.

Materials: None.

1-1	Choose a difficult situation from your work, for example a situation in which you are teaching. Imagine yourself back in this situation. **Write down:** • What are you thinking? • Why are you thinking this? • What or who decides what you think? • How do your thoughts influence your experience in this situation?
2-2	Exchange, and help each other to reconstruct your thoughts in this situation. Be critical towards each other, for what you are thinking is not always obvious. Someone else could be thinking something different in the same situation. Would you also be able to think differently about the situation? Would this affect the outcome of the situation? Change roles after four minutes.
3-1	**Write down:** • Does 'what' and 'how' you think help you in this situation? • If so, why? If not, why not? • Observe the space that is being freed up when you let go of the negative thoughts (which core quality can help you to do this?). Can you look differently at the situation now in a way that helps you to deal with it better?
4-2	Exchange.
5-G	Discuss with the group, paying attention to how you can deal with your own thoughts in a way that helps to improve your experience in the situation. Write down an intention you have at this point.
6-1	Choose a situation in your week ahead in which you will be actively doing something and want to start paying attention to the effect of your (positive and negative) thoughts.

Write down:
- What situation did you choose?
- How are you going observe your own thinking?
- What do you want to learn from these observations?
- How will you report your observations?

7-G	Discuss, paying attention to how to observe this specific situation.

19 Observing Your Thinking

Thinking is like a wave in constant motion, which can shift from one moment to the other. Restless thoughts can be the root of stress. These thoughts don't help you to function optimally: they limit your power. When your thinking is more peaceful, you can reduce stress and increase your power. The following activity helps you to become aware of how fickle and volatile your thinking often is. This helps you to understand whether and how you can choose to bring more peace into your thoughts.

Observing Your Thinking		
Goal: Becoming aware of chaotic thought patterns versus focused thoughts. **Materials:** Pen and paper, a timer (stopwatch).	1-1	Usually your mind doesn't stop. It jumps from one thought to the next. This usually happens unconsciously. In this exercise you will try to look at how your thoughts jump around and how this affects you. Of course, the act of doing this exercise influences your normal thought patterns, but it will still help you to understand how this works. Take a piece of paper and a pen. Set a timer for five minutes. Take a few deep breaths and relax. Write down a keyword for each thought that comes up. Relax again—take another deep breath in, and out—and set your intention to let go of the thoughts.
	2-2	After five minutes: Exchange what you notice when you observe your thoughts for a while.
	3-G	Discuss with the group: What do you observe, and what is the effect of your thoughts?
	4-1	**Write down:** • Can you stop thinking completely if that is your intention? • If so, how do you do this and what does it give you? If not, what happens and what is the effect?

		• To what extent can observing your thoughts be a way to get more peace and focus? • Which core qualities can help you to have more peace and focus?
	5-2	Exchange. What are the benefits of observing your thinking? Which core qualities help to achieve peace and focus?
	6-G	Discuss with the group: What helps you to achieve more peace and focus? (e.g. no resistance, acceptance, direction, openness, being in the here-and-now, applying core qualities such as peace or willpower).
	7-1	What are the concrete actions you can take to make your thoughts less jumpy and achieve more peace? **Write down:** Which core qualities will you start applying to achieve this?

20   Developing More Focused Thinking

Clarity and sharpness in thinking increases your power. Focusing your thoughts will sometimes work for shorter or longer periods, but sometimes doesn't work at all. In this activity you will observe what effect focused thoughts have on you and what you can do to develop and direct this focus.

Developing More Focused Thinking		
Goal: Becoming aware of the importance of focused thinking; analyzing the difference between focused and chaotic thinking. **Materials:** Paper.	1-1	Go back to a positive teaching situation or other situation from your work in which you were focused on *one* thing. **Write down:** • How do you experience this focus? What is its effect? • Does having a focus have advantages and disadvantages? • Can you make a drawing of how focus works? • Now, make another drawing that represents chaotic thought patterns.
	2-2	Exchange and discuss the difference between chaotic and focused thinking. Discuss the advantages and disadvantages.

3-G	Discuss with the group: • What is focus, and what is the difference between focused and chaotic thinking? • How often do you have a focus in your work or studies? • What is improved by having a focus? (Think of clear goals, challenges, time pressure, an interest that is at stake, your willpower, and so forth.)
4-1	What can you do to improve your focus in situations in which this is important? **Write down:** • Which core quality helps you to have more focus? • How will you apply this core quality in the next hour to maintain a targeted focus?
5-2	Exchange. Which core qualities will you apply?
6-G	Which core qualities help you to have focus? (e.g. direction, willpower, being in touch with the here-and-now). Feel these core qualities within you.
7-1	**Write down:** • What will you do this week to pay attention to having a focus in your activities? • Which core qualities will you apply this week to increase your focus? • How will you decide whether this works or not?
8-G	Briefly discuss and help each other to clarify specific actions.

21 Looking at a Problem through Different 'Glasses'

Your mind is optimally used when you look at things through different perspectives ('glasses'). By doing this, you often become clearer and have unexpected insights.

Looking at a Problem through Different 'Glasses'		
Goal: Using different ways of thinking to solve a problem. **Materials:** None.	1-1	Visualize a problem or difficult situation you want to solve. You will look at this through six different glasses.[1] **Write down:** • *The white glasses.* What are the facts (objective— without interpretation or your own opinion)? • *The yellow glasses.* What is positive and constructive, what are positive opportunities, what are the values and advantages?

• *The red glasses.* What does your intuition tell you?
• *The black glasses.* What do you have to be careful about, what are the negative aspects, disadvantages, and opportunities for errors?
• *The green glasses.* What is the creative potential, which new ideas are presented, how can you move beyond the known, move your boundaries?
• *The blue glasses.* How do you maintain your overview of the situation, how to you maintain distance and control, how do you draw conclusions?

2-2	Exchange how you used the different glasses to look at your problem. What was it like to use these different glasses? Which ones were easy and which were difficult for you?
3-G	Discuss with the group.
4-1	**Write down:** • What did you achieve by looking at your problem through these six glasses? • What core qualities did you use? • Which of these glasses do you use less in your normal thinking and analyzing of problems?
5-2	**Exchange.** • What did you achieve with this activity? • What core qualities do you apply regularly and which ones could you apply more? • What core qualities are linked to the different glasses? (e.g. objectivity, optimism, sensitivity, caution, creativity, being organized).
6-G	Brief discussion with the whole group.
7-1	**Write down:** • What core qualities can help you to improve your way of solving a problem or difficult situation? • What can you do to apply this core quality (more often)?

1   De Bono (1985) uses these six approaches to utilize the power of thoughts in solving problems. What we call 'glasses' in this book, he calls 'hats' you can put on.

22   Discerning Differences Among Feelings

Up until now we have focused on *thinking*. This next series of activities focuses on *feeling*. Central to this is how you observe your feelings and what type of information these feelings and emotions contain. How do you deal with this information? These activities also help you gain insight into the differences in emotions and how they affect your life.

We will start with an activity that helps you to make contact with all sorts of feelings that can appear in your life (and work). You will see how feelings can sometimes be subtly different or at other times extremely different.[1] It may also become clear how various people respond differently to situations. Moreover, you can experience that people sometimes use the same feeling-word but have a different feeling associated with it.

Discerning Differences Among Feelings

Goal: Observing the differences between feelings and comparing the energy of the different feelings.

Materials: 'Feeling quadrants' form (Figure 3.2, see @, pdf #30), table of 'feeling words' (Table 3.1, see @, pdf #26). It is possible to make cards with the various feeling words and put them on the form 'feeling quadrants,' or Table 3.1 can be used for finding feeling words that can be written on the form.

1-1 Put the form 'feeling quadrants' (Figure 3.2) in front of you. On the right of the horizontal line is 'positive' and on the left 'negative.' Decide for yourself what this means. The vertical line runs from 'passive' to 'active.' This creates four squares (quadrants).
Choose a feeling-word from the feeling cards (see also Table 3.1). Experience this feeling within yourself (if necessary, return to a situation in which you had this feeling).
Write down the feeling in one of the quadrants on the form with a pencil. Continue in the same way with the next feeling, until you have gone through all the feelings. Compare the feelings with each other. You can add any additional feelings to the table if necessary.

2-2 Compare and discuss your findings. Pay attention to similarities and differences in your groupings. Discuss how you experience feelings differently.

3-1 **Write down:**
• What do you notice about your groupings?
• How did you separate the feelings from each other? (Describe accurately how you observed these differences.)
• How do the four quadrants differ to you?
• What is the effect of more or less active/passive (the vertical line)?
• What is the effect of positive and negative feelings (the horizontal line)?

4-2 Discuss the points from step 3-1 in pairs.

---

1 The use of the four quadrants to note the differences between feelings is based on research by Altarriba, Basnight, and Canary (2003) and Russell (1980).

5-G	Discuss in the whole group, focusing on:
	• Observing feelings and the differences in observations between people.
	• What type of information do feelings give? What do you do with this in your life and work?
	• How do you feel your feelings? (How does that work in you?)
	• How can people experience the same feeling-word differently?
	• What is the meaning of the concepts 'negative' and 'positive' and the concepts 'passive' and 'active'?
6-1	**Write down:**
	How will you pay attention in the coming week to feelings that you have in certain situations, and your reactions to these feelings?

Happy	Delighted	Excited
Astonished	Aroused	Tense
Alarmed	Angry	Afraid
Annoyed	Distressed	Frustrated
Miserable	Sad	Gloomy
Depressed	Bored	Droopy
Tired	Sleepy	Calm
Relaxed	Satisfied	At ease
Content	Serene	Glad
Pleased	....	....

Table 3.1   Feeling words (based on Russell, 1980)

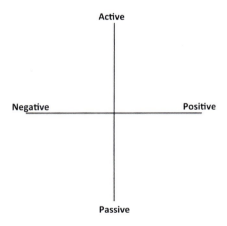

Figure 3.2   Feeling quadrants

23   Becoming Aware of the Effects of Your Feelings

This activity is a continuation of the previous activity. This time the goal is to become more aware of what your feelings are telling you. This exercise can also help you to observe how your feelings correspond with your thinking, wanting, and doing.

Becoming Aware of the Effects of Your Feelings		
This activity is a continuation of Activity 22: Discerning Differences Between Feelings.		
Goal: Feeling your feelings and observing (subtle) differences; comparing the energy of feelings and finding the right words for them; recognizing and verbalizing patterns in your feelings.	1-1	Place the sheet with the feeling quadrants and the feeling words in front of you. Choose from each quadrant a feeling that you experience frequently (in your work or your personal life). **Write down:** • Which feelings did you choose? • When or where do you have these feelings? • What effect do these feelings have on you?
	2-2	Share your insights and help each other to deepen these insights. Pay attention to the effects that the feelings have on you.
Materials: Completed form 'Feeling quadrants' with feeling words from previous exercise (@, pdf #30), form 'Comparing four feelings' (@, pdf #31).	3-G	Discussion in the group. Focus on: • When and where do these feelings occur? • What do these feelings tell you? • What information do they contain? • What is your reaction to these feelings?
	4-1	Take the form 'Comparing four feelings,' which has on it the four columns, and write in each of the columns one of your chosen words. Answer the questions for each feeling.
	5-2	Exchange and help each other to increase your understanding and to answer the questions as accurately as possible.
	6-1	**Write down:** • What have you noticed about the relationship between feeling, thinking, and wanting? • What insights are you gaining? • Is there something you would like to change or develop in how you relate to your feeling, thinking, and wanting? If so, what and how?
	7-G	Discussion in the whole group. Focus on making intentions explicit.

Feeling 1	Feeling 2	Feeling 3	Feeling 4
Situations in which I have this feeling are:	Situations in which I have this feeling are:	Situations in which I have this feeling are:	Situations in which I have this feeling are:
When I feel this I **think**:	When I feel this I **think**:	When I feel this I **think**:	When I feel this I **think**:
When I feel this I **do**:	When I feel this I **do**:	When I feel this I **do**:	When I feel this I **do**:
When I feel this I **want to**:	When I feel this I **want to**:	When I feel this I **want to**:	When I feel this I **want to**:
What strikes me in comparing my responses:	What strikes me in comparing my responses:	What strikes me in comparing my responses:	What strikes me in comparing my responses:

Form 'Comparing four feelings'

24 Deepening Contact by Using the Elevator between Thinking, Feeling, and Wanting

As we saw earlier, thinking, feeling, and wanting are three different and indispensable information channels. When you are really paying attention to the information in these channels, you can make optimal use of your full potential. We call this 'using the elevator': switching between thinking, feeling, and wanting. In western culture, the focus is usually on thinking. There is a tendency to exclude feeling and wanting from our awareness, and it may be difficult to really engage your feeling and wanting when you are in a discussion or at work. However, if you can do this, it will make you much better at your work. It helps you to really connect to your qualities and power. The following activities will help you to learn or improve how to use the elevator.

This activity has been designed for pair work, and it focuses on creating a balance between thinking, feeling, and wanting when you are in a conversation. Most people are not very used to this, but in general, teachers will be fairly in touch with their feelings and those of their students because children do this very naturally and, as a result, also evoke this in the teacher. However, when communicating with colleagues or administrators, many teachers are inclined to function from the mind. Discussions are conducted using habitual patterns, in which the thinking is generally more pronounced. In this case, feeling and wanting rarely come into play, or they occur as background information. Unfortunately, this will mean that a lot of important information gets lost. It can also lead to a lack of true connection between people.

In the following activity you will put the elevator into practice in a conversation. You will try to consciously apply thinking, feeling, and wanting while you are in this conversation. We will use cards to help you with this. This can initially seem quite artificial, but that is always the case with new things. Try to see beyond that and ask yourself what impact using the elevator has on the depth of the conversation. Do you get more information? Is there more potential? Does it achieve something? And if so, what?

Deepening Contact by Using the Elevator between Thinking, Feeling, and Wanting		
Goal: Developing competency at switching between thinking, feeling, and wanting. **Materials:** Cards with questions about thinking, feeling, and wanting (@, pdf #2 or #3), Figure 'The Elevator' (Figure 3.1, pdf #16).	1-1	Remember an inspiring teaching situation or another inspiring situation from your work.
	2-2	**Divide the roles (A and B).** A reflects on an inspiring experience. B puts the elevator cards (with thinking, feeling, and wanting questions) in front of him/her in three piles, and for each question chooses one card. Choose a card from another pile for each new question, in the order thinking—feeling—wanting—thinking, and so on. Take a moment for each question to experience the difference between thinking, feeling, and wanting, and the type of information you get from each type of question. Try to keep speed in working through the cards (but don't go too fast).
	3-G	Discuss in the group: how are you doing? • What are the differences in the conversations depending on whether you are focusing on thinking, feeling, or wanting? • What is the difference for the person reflecting? And for the person asking questions? • Is there a difference in the information you receive from thinking, feeling, or wanting?
	4-1	Now go back to a negative teaching situation or another negative work situation.

5-2	**Divide roles again (A and B).** A speaks. B puts the elevator cards in front of them in three piles, asks a question, and for each question chooses one card. Choose a new pile for each new question. Try to keep speed in working through the cards (but don't go too fast).
6-G	Discussion: • What is the difference between asking further questions about a positive or negative work experience? • What is achieved by switching between thinking, feeling, and wanting? • How does this improve your own self-awareness and connection with others? • How would you like to take this insight forward? • How can you keep practicing this until it is a habit?

It is possible to gradually increase the difficulty of this activity:

Level 1: Use the cards with the pre-printed questions for thinking, feeling, and wanting (with the colors yellow for thinking, blue for feeling, and red for wanting) (see @, pdf #2 or #3).

How does this affect you? Using the elevator - short Feeling 3	**Formulate your own feeling question.** Using the elevator - short Feeling 4
What are you thinking? Using the elevator - short Thinking 1	**What do you think about this?** Using the elevator - short Thinking 1

Example of 'Using the elevator' cards, short version

Level 2: Use a combination of pre-printed questions and blank, colored cards (with the indications for thinking, feeling, and wanting on them) (see @, pdf #3 and #4).

Level 3: Only use the blank, colored cards (indicating thinking, feeling, and wanting) (see pdf #4), while the person who is asking the questions thinks of their own questions.

Level 4: Do the 'placemats activity.' Make 'placemats' on letter-size paper (pdf #32), which you put down on the floor: one for thinking, one for feeling, and one for wanting. Each time the attention changes from one to the other, the speaker steps onto the appropriate placemat.

Level 5: Don't use any tools, but do focus on using the elevator.

25 Managing the Difference between 'Wanting' and 'Having to'

'Wanting' and 'having to' are very closely related. What is the difference and what is the effect of this difference? The following activity will help you to discover that.

Managing the Difference Between 'Wanting' and 'Having to'		
Goal: Experiencing the subtle differences between wanting and having to; becoming aware of the choices you have and the role of core values.	1-1	Look at the scale of wanting (Figure 3.3). **Write down:** • Three examples of choices you make from inside (which come close to ten). • Three examples of neutral choices (around five). • Three examples of choices you really made against your will (around zero).
Materials: Scale of wanting (Figure 3.3, see also @, pdf #18). Potentially also the 'Core qualities' cards (see @, pdf #6).	2-2	Discuss how each type of choice (for zero, five, and ten on the scale) affects you. • What is the difference in energy? • How do you experience 'having to' versus 'wanting'? • How do you know whether you really want something or not? How do you find out?
	3-G	Discussion that builds on these last points. An interesting point of discussion is also: How do you know whether you really want something or not, and how do you find out?

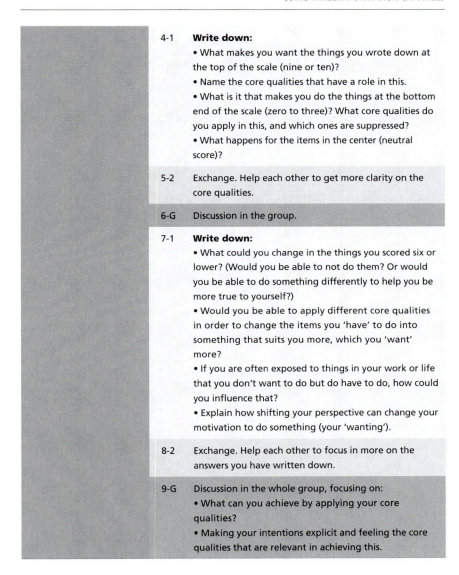

4-1	**Write down:** • What makes you want the things you wrote down at the top of the scale (nine or ten)? • Name the core qualities that have a role in this. • What is it that makes you do the things at the bottom end of the scale (zero to three)? What core qualities do you apply in this, and which ones are suppressed? • What happens for the items in the center (neutral score)?
5-2	Exchange. Help each other to get more clarity on the core qualities.
6-G	Discussion in the group.
7-1	**Write down:** • What could you change in the things you scored six or lower? (Would you be able to not do them? Or would you be able to do something differently to help you be more true to yourself?) • Would you be able to apply different core qualities in order to change the items you 'have' to do into something that suits you more, which you 'want' more? • If you are often exposed to things in your work or life that you don't want to do but do have to do, how could you influence that? • Explain how shifting your perspective can change your motivation to do something (your 'wanting').
8-2	Exchange. Help each other to focus in more on the answers you have written down.
9-G	Discussion in the whole group, focusing on: • What can you achieve by applying your core qualities? • Making your intentions explicit and feeling the core qualities that are relevant in achieving this.

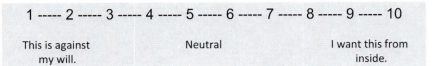

1 ----- 2 ----- 3 ----- 4 ----- 5 ----- 6 ----- 7 ----- 8 ----- 9 ----- 10

| This is against my will. | Neutral | I want this from inside. |

Figure 3.3 The scale of wanting

26 Using Your Willpower

Your will is something you can apply very well when it comes to realizing an ideal or dream. When you do this, a creative energy is released which starts to move you into the direction you really want to go. This creative power will be larger if your will is more powerful and your focus clearer. Therefore, it is very important to translate what you really want into new habits and apply these in your life.

Using Your Willpower		
Goal: Directing your will towards an ideal; experiencing how this affects you. **Materials:** None.	1-1	Turn your attention to an ideal or desire, something you really want to make happen. **Write down:** • What is it you want *exactly*? Describe this very clearly. • Why do you want this? What is the reason? • Make the image of what you want crystal clear, concrete, and real.
	2-2	Exchange and help each other to clarify the image and reason for your ideal as much as possible. Look together at the obstacles that come up and try to solve them by revisiting your ideal and making contact with its core qualities.
	3-G	Exchange and ask the question: What is it that you really want? Try to bridge this issue to the theme 'focus' (see Activity 20).
	4-1	**Write down:** • My ideal is . . . • I will take **the following real steps** to achieve this . . . (for example, new behavior you will adopt) • I will apply the following core qualities . . .
	5-2	Discuss what you have written down and help each other to make this as clear as possible, to feel it strongly, and to feel that something is being set in motion.
	6-G	Exchange. What does it feel like to give all the energy you can to an ideal or wish? It is crucial to translate this energy into concrete actions. How could you go about doing this? How would you support yourself in this?

7-1   Visualize the outcome of your ideal and consciously maintain this image as sharply and clearly as possible.
Write down:
What are the concrete things you will do to realize your ideal?

27   Working and Living from Your Passion

There can be many reasons for you to want something in your (work) life. We started exploring this in the previous exercise. When something you really want is in harmony with who you truly are (your core), we call this *harmonic passion* (Vallerand *et al.*, 2003). In such a case, we say that you have a calling or mission. But there can also be limiting aspects to your passion. There could be a pressure to do something, perhaps because you are addicted to the pressure. Another thing that can happen is that you act from expectations you have unconsciously adopted, for example: trying to achieve something at all cost, working to achieve a certain status, or doing something to get others' approval. We call this *obsessive passion*. This obsession can almost blind you to the truth.

Working and Living from Your Passion		
Goal: Becoming aware of your passion and the extent to which this comes from your core, or as an expression of something else. **Materials:** None.	1-1	**Write down:** • What are your inspirations in your (work) life? What drives you? • What is really your passion (in your work)? • Which core qualities can you recognize in your passion?
	2-2	Exchange and make contact. What are the core qualities in your passion?
	3-G	Discuss with the whole group. Focus on the topic of what really comes from inside. Could there also be some restriction in your passion? A feeling of having to do it at all costs?
	4-1	**Write down:** • Are there moments where something you are passionate about becomes forced, an obsessive passion? For example, this could be working too long, holding on to something too tight, not having perspective anymore, forcing something, not being able to let go, ending up 'having to' do it, and so forth. • What happens then? What do you want then? What does this achieve? • Which core qualities help you to create a balance?

5-2 Exchange your reflections.
• Discuss obsessive passion. What happens when you are in that state? What is it you want? What does it achieve for you?
• Which core qualities help you to turn an obsessive passion into a harmonic passion?

6-1 **Write down:**
• What do you get out of harmonic passion?
• What is the contrast between harmonic and obsessive passion?
• Pay attention this week to the passion in your life and the passion in the lives of some of the people around you. Try to distinguish between harmonic and obsessive passion.
• Finally, which core qualities could help you to avoid obsessive passion?

SCIENTIFIC BACKGROUND

Thinking, Feeling, and Wanting

Thinking, feeling, and wanting can be seen as fundamental functions of the human organism (Järvilehto, 2001; see also Klein, Rozendal, & Cosmides, 2002). Järvilehto (2001) states: "Intellect, will, and heart are descriptions of the fundamental aspects of the organism-environment system; 'intellect' (knowledge) being the quality of its structure, 'will' (motivation) the direction of its basic activity, and 'heart' (emotion) the quality of the reorganization." Kim, Chan, and Chan (2007) state that at the root of human desire is a complex interaction between thinking and feeling. Wegner and Wheatley (1999, 2003) discuss how the will operates and they indicate that much of what we humans want is directed by outside influences and happens unconsciously (Bargh, 1990; Bargh & Barndollar, 1996; Bargh & Chartrand 1999; Bargh & Ferguson, 2000).

The Experiential System and Rational System

When we take a closer look at the background mechanisms in people, research by Epstein (1990) is fundamental. He proposes that in the human consciousness there are systems that interact and run in parallel. The two key ones are the *rational system* and the *experiential system*.

The *rational system* operates on a conscious level; it is analytical and logical. The rational system is specific and detailed, uses abstractions (for example in the form of language), and it can make conscious decisions and connections. The rational system is comparatively slow compared to the *experiential system*. The latter functions largely via emotions and images. It is closely linked to physical responses and automatic processes. It is very fast and not linked to language. It functions without the conscious attention of the person (Epstein, 1990, p. 168; Epstein, 1998a, 1998b see also Bargh, 1990; Bargh & Barndollar, 1996; Bargh & Chartrand, 1999). The experiential system functions holistically. This means that the world is experienced as coherent 'wholes,' in which cognitive and emotional aspects are merged.

The rational and experience-based systems are closely connected and operate in parallel. In other words, experiences influence the rational system. This includes the thoughts and judgments we have. But the rational system can in turn also affect and adjust the experience-based system. For example, a negative experience may influence the experience-based system to take actions such as stepping back emotionally, or doing nothing and waiting, but the rational system can nevertheless choose to carry on. Epstein's theory brings clarity to the fact that there are strong connections between thinking, feeling, and action.

Brain Research

Neurophysiologic research has shown the tight relationship between thinking and feeling as the source of our actions. Based on findings from their brain research, Immordino-Yang and Damasio (2007) state that the majority of our thinking occurs through processes in the brain in which thinking and feeling are closely connected. Damasio and his team have done extensive research in this field. He has showed that people constantly feel things but are not always aware of this (see for example Damasio, 1999).

Positive and Negative Feelings

Frederickson emphasizes in her research that positive feelings are beneficial to people (Fredrickson, 2001). Positive feelings broaden your perception, while negative feelings restrict it. Positive feelings create a buffer of energy which can be used in difficult times ('resource building'), while negative feelings take energy (Frederickson, 1998, p. 312).

Positive feelings also make people more creative (Fredrickson, 2009; see also Skinner & Edge, 2002) and help them to learn more easily and quickly. People can learn to have a positive approach when dealing with setbacks. For this, it is important not to focus too much on what is not going well and why this is the case, but to make use of the psychological capital that is present inside.

Positive Intentions

Research shows that positive thoughts, expectations, and intentions do really create more positive results than intentions that are based on doubt or fear (Taylor, Kemeny, Reed, Bower, & Gruenewald, 2000). However, it is important that the positive intention is also expressed in (new) behavior, otherwise it has limited results (Webb & Sheeran, 2006). It is therefore very important to formulate concrete intentions about changing behavior that are focused on the desired results.

4 Using the Power of Your Desires and Ideals

> Debby is a teacher. There is something missing for her in the team of teachers at her school. She is looking for personal contact, but the communication is business-like and lacking this connection. What she would really like is to work from a feeling of togetherness. However, the way the team is functioning right now affects her work in a negative way. She retreats to working with the students more; with them it is easier to have this personal contact. She doesn't enjoy her work enough now, which affects her involvement with the team and the quality of the work she is providing for them.

In the previous chapter, we discussed that people are constantly thinking and feeling. At the same time, they are also constantly 'wanting.' We already paid attention to this 'wanting' in Chapter 3, but we will elaborate on it further in this fourth chapter, because the 'will' has an important role in one's development. 'Wanting' shows up very clearly in people's needs. People's actions are considerably influenced by their needs. This has led large organizations, such as schools, educational institutions, and companies to pay more attention to the needs of their employees. Their needs are not just a requirement for their sense of well-being, but also for their effectiveness at work. This is why it is important to recognize your own needs.

28 Introductory Activity: Knowing Your Needs

What are needs really? Into what direction does a need send you? How does this need enter into your thinking and feeling and into what you are doing? The following activity will help you explore this.

Introductory Activity: Knowing Your Needs

Goal: Recognizing your needs in a work situation. **Materials:** None.	1-1	Remember a difficult or negative situation from your work, for example a teaching situation.
	2-1	Visualize yourself back in this situation. **Write down:** • Where does this situation occur? • *What do you feel?* Is this the feeling you would like to have? If not, what is it that you need? • *What are you thinking?* Are these thoughts ones you like to think? If not, what is it that you need? • *What do you do?* Is this what you enjoy doing? If not, what is it that you need?
	3-1	What clarity did you get about your needs in this situation?

When we talk about the basic needs of people, this generally comes down to three types of needs: (a) material needs; (b) psychological needs; and (c) the need for a feeling of purpose, which can also be referred to as the need for self-actualization. We will elaborate on these three types of needs below.

a)   Material Needs

In their needs around work, people can, for example, have a wish to have a good salary. Teachers often wish for a comfortable classroom, up-to-date materials, and adequate support. Others would be happier if they had their own office, with a telephone and a computer. What stands out here is that material needs are very important for people, but are also transient and can change rapidly. Once you have a computer in your classroom, you would like a smart board, and very quickly after that you realize it would be nice for all students to have a laptop or tablet that they can use at school. But this then leads to your desire for them to have a quiet workspace where they can do group work. When these don't materialize, this may become a major disappointment. Suddenly you are not so happy with the facilities that you have. In other words, the satisfaction of material needs doesn't seem to make people happy in the long term.

b)   Psychological Needs

Now we will look at the second category of needs: psychological needs.

29 Introductory Activity: Recognizing Your Basic Psychological Needs

Research has shown that people have three main psychological needs (Deci & Ryan, 1985, 2000), which are therefore called the *basic psychological needs*:

- *Competence*, the feeling of being in control of the world around you.
- *Autonomy*, the feeling of being able to direct your own life.
- *Relatedness*, the feeling of being connected to others and having positive relationships.

The following activity will help you to discover what the fulfillment of your basic psychological needs means for you. Table 4.1 shows a few questions from each of three subscales in the Basic Needs Satisfaction at Work Questionnaire (Deci *et al.*, 2011). Please go to www.selfdeterminationtheory.org to answer all 21 items on the questionnaire and then complete the activity that follows Table 4.1.

The following questions concern your feelings about your job during the last year. (If you have been on this job for less than a year, this concerns the entire time you have been at this job.) Please indicate how true each of the following statements is for you given your experiences on this job. Remember that your boss will never know how you responded to the questions. Please use the following scale in responding to the items.

1		2	3	4		5	6	7
not at all true				somewhat true				very true

When I am at work:

1. I feel like I can make a lot of inputs to deciding how my job gets done. 1 2 3 4 5 6 7
2. I really like the people I work with. 1 2 3 4 5 6 7
3. I do not feel very competent when I am at work. 1 2 3 4 5 6 7
4. People at work tell me I am good at what I do. 1 2 3 4 5 6 7
5. I feel pressured at work. 1 2 3 4 5 6 7
6. I get along with people at work. 1 2 3 4 5 6 7

Scoring Information

Form three subscale scores by averaging item responses for each subscale after reverse scoring the items that were worded in the negative direction. Specifically, any item that has (R) after it in the code below should be reverse scored by subtracting the person's response from 8.

Autonomy: items 1, 5(R), . . .
Competence: items 3(R), 4, . . .
Relatedness: items 2, 6, . . .

Table 4.1 Basic needs satisfaction at work questionnaire

Please note that only the full questionnaire will provide your score, as this is an excerpt. To give you an indication on what a score means once you have completed the full questionnaire, you can see a high score on each scale (Autonomy > 39, Competence > 34, Relatedness > 45) as an indication of fulfillment of the three basic psychological needs, a lower score on each scale indicates thwarting of these needs.

Note: This questionnaire is reprinted in shortened form with permission from Dr. Edward Deci. For more information, see www.selfdeterminationtheory.org.

Table 4.1 Continued

Introductory Activity: Recognizing Your Basic Psychological Needs		
Goal: Recognizing basic psychological needs. **Materials:** Questionnaire 'Basic needs satisfaction at work' (www.selfdeterminationtheory.org).	1-1	Complete the questionnaire on *Basic needs satisfaction at work* (www.selfdeterminationtheory.org) for a difficult work or learning situation, for example in a classroom or in collaborating with colleagues.
	2-1	What is your score for: • Competence? • Autonomy? • Relatedness?
	3-1	**Write down:** • What is your need for competence in this situation? • What is your need for autonomy in this situation? • What is your need for relatedness in this situation? • For each of these three basic needs, what is the effect on you when they are under pressure?
	4-1	Now complete the questionnaire while thinking about a very positive work or learning experience. • What is the difference? • What effect does it have on you when each of these three basic needs is fulfilled?

c)   The Need for a Feeling of Purpose: The area of ideals

People want their lives to be meaningful, to add something to the world that is valuable to others or themselves. In many professions this is the most important drive for people. For people who work in education, this is often strongly connected to making contact with students and feeling able to contribute to their development and life. But people in the welfare or social sector strongly recognize this need as well. Really, this is the same for all professions; people are constantly looking for the 'usefulness' of their work. You could say that once you find a purpose in your work you start to enjoy it.

This takes us to the area of ideals. People aspire to achieve certain goals, consciously or unconsciously. They have some idea of the ideal situation they would like to achieve. This can be about 'small ideals,' for example, to bring a task to a good end. However, it can also be about 'big' ideals which give meaning to one's existence. For one person it could be important to travel the world, for someone else it could be important to contribute to a better world, and for someone else again it could be to teach people something that will be useful for them, and so forth.

So, in this third type, it is really about ideals that go beyond the everyday issues, which makes this area the most fundamental of all. People want to be able to see the effect of their work or life as part of a larger whole. At first, some ideals might not seem related to issues such as purposefulness. In examples such as travelling the world or earning a lot of money, it can be difficult to see the connection with purposefulness, but it may still be there. Someone might want to travel the world to get a better understanding of different cultures or to get a broader perspective on life. When someone would really like to earn a lot of money, this might have ideals behind it such as being able to enjoy life or realizing a better life for their family.

Ideals and core qualities are closely related. If your ideal is to make people happy, you are likely to have a strongly developed core quality of compassion. If your ideal is to create something very beautiful, you are often creative. If your ideal is that everything at work is well organized, you will often be accurate, and so forth. In short, ideals stimulate you to develop certain core qualities. Therefore, it is very important that you are aware of your ideals as they shape the direction of your professional development.

We can also reverse this. Your core qualities can make you feel a strong desire to use these qualities in the world as well as you can, or said differently, your core qualities help to shape your ideals. We can also say that people strive to make optimal use of their personal psychological capital. This striving is one's 'natural ideal.' The term self-actualization is used to express the growth process through which someone's natural potential continues to be further developed and applied. For many people, self-actualization is the only thing that gives them a feeling of fulfillment, the feeling of expressing themselves fully. The needs of this third type (c) go beyond material needs (a) and basic psychological needs (b). Only when (a) and (b) are fulfilled is there room to address (c).

FURTHER EXPLORATION

You are completely empowered when you feel successful, when you experience that you can do what you really want to do yourself and, at the same time, also feel connected to other people. In this case the three basic psychological needs are fulfilled: the need for competence, autonomy, and relatedness. Even though these three are different, their fulfillment is strongly related. When one basic need has been fulfilled, there is a bigger chance that the other two will also be fulfilled. The opposite is also true. To really discover the difference between the three basic psychological needs, we have listed a series of exercises in which you focus solely on *one* of the three basic psychological needs. This will help you to recognize them and find out whether they are fulfilled or suppressed.

30 Discovering the Connection between Fulfillment of the Need for Competence and Success in Your Work

This activity helps you to look at your need for competence. What effect does it have on you when this is fulfilled or suppressed? What can you do to experience more fulfillment of this need? For a school principal this could be feeling that you really direct the development in your school. For a teacher this could be to have a feeling of competence in teaching or interacting with a class. For your feeling of competence it is important that you experience for yourself that you are functioning well and that you are feeling competent in the situation, given the potential and materials that you have at that time.

Discovering the Connection between Fulfillment of the Need for Competence and Success in Your Work		
Goal: Experiencing and verbalizing the effect of fulfillment and suppression of the need for competence. **Materials:** Sticky notes (red and green).	1-1	Remember a situation in which you felt very successful, in which you were able to do things well. Take a (green) sticky note. **Write on it:** • What did you do? • How successful were you at it? • How did you feel? • What did you think? • What did you want?

2-2	Exchange. Help each other to clearly verbalize what you thought, felt, and wanted in this successful situation.
3-1	Remember a situation in which you felt you were failing, in which you were not able to do something. Take a (red) sticky note. **Write on it:** • What did you do? • How successful were you at it? • How did you feel? • What did you think? • What did you want?
4-2	Exchange. Help each other to clearly verbalize what you thought, felt, and wanted in this situation.
5-4	Compare in your group of four what you have written down about your thinking, feeling, and wanting in the two situations. **One of you writes down:** According to your group of four, what are the characteristic thoughts and feelings when the need for competence is fulfilled? What are the characteristic thoughts and feelings when this need for competence is suppressed?
6-G	Discussion in the whole group. Focus on: How realistic, useful, and helpful are the negative reactions? What would be more useful?
7-1	**Write down:** • What core qualities can you use to be less affected if the need for competence is suppressed in a difficult situation? • What are the concrete things you can do to use this/these core quality/qualities?
8-G	Discuss concrete plans to use these core qualities.

31 Discovering the Connection between Fulfillment of the Need for Autonomy and Motivation in Your Work

The following activity will help you to look at your need for autonomy. For example, what is the effect on you and your work when you do or don't feel autonomous?

Discovering the Connection between Fulfillment of the Need for Autonomy and Motivation in Your Work

Goal: Experiencing and verbalizing the effect of fulfillment and suppression of the need for autonomy.

Materials: Sticky notes (red and green).

1-1 Remember a work situation, for example in teaching or in a staff meeting, in which you were completely yourself, able to express your ideas, and were being heard.
Take a (green) sticky note.
Write down:
• What did you do?
• How did that work?
• How did you feel?
• What did you think?
• What did you want?

2-2 Exchange. Help each other to verbalize what you thought, felt, and wanted in this situation.

3-1 Remember a situation in your work in which you felt you were hardly or not at all able to express yourself, in which you had to do something you didn't want to.
Take a (red) sticky note.
Write down:
• What did you do?
• How did that go?
• How did you feel?
• What did you think?
• What did you want?

4-2 Exchange. Help each other to verbalize what you thought, felt, and wanted in this situation.

5-4 Compare in your group of four what you have written down about your thinking, feeling, and wanting in these two situations.
One of you writes down:
According to your group, what are the characteristic thoughts and feelings for the fulfillment of the need for autonomy?
What are the characteristic thoughts and feelings when the need for autonomy is suppressed?

6-G Discuss with the whole group. Focus on: How realistic, useful, and helpful are the negative reactions? What would be more useful?

7-1	**Write down:** • Which core qualities can you use in a difficult situation to be less affected by the suppression of your need for autonomy? • What concrete things can you do to use this/these core quality/qualities?
8-G	Discuss concrete plans to use these core qualities.

32 Discovering the Relationship between Fulfillment of the Need for Relatedness and Having Contact

The following activity helps you to look at your need for relatedness and what effect it has on you and your work when this need is suppressed or fulfilled.

Discovering the Relationship between Fulfillment of the Need for Relatedness and Having Contact		
Goal: Experiencing and verbalizing the effect of fulfillment and suppression of the need for relatedness. **Materials:** Sticky notes (red and green).	1-1	Remember a work situation, for example a situation with students or colleagues, in which you felt very connected to others. Take a green sticky note. **Write down:** • Who were you with? • What did you do? • How did you feel? • What did you think? • What did you want?
	2-2	Exchange. Help each other to clearly describe what you think, feel, and want in a situation like this.
	3-1	Remember a work situation, for example a situation with students or colleagues in which you felt little or no connection with others. Take a red sticky note. **Write down:** • Who were you with? • What did you do? • How did you feel? • What did you think? • What did you want?

	4-2	Exchange. Help each other to clearly describe what you thought, felt, and wanted in a situation like this.
	5-4	Compare in your group of four what you have written down about your thinking, feeling, and wanting in the two situations. **One of you writes down:** • According to your group of four, what are the characteristic thoughts and feelings when the need for relatedness is fulfilled? • What are the characteristic thoughts and feelings when the need for relatedness is suppressed? • What does all of this have to do with 'contact'?
	6-G	Discussion with the whole group. Focus on: How realistic, useful, and helpful are the negative reactions? What would be more useful?
	7-1	**Write down:** • What core qualities can help you to be less affected by the suppression of the need for relatedness in a difficult situation? • What concrete things can you do to use this/these core quality/qualities?
	8-G	Discuss concrete plans to use these core qualities.

33   Being More Successful at Work by Feeling More Competent

Fulfilling all three basic needs is an essential ingredient in being able to work and live well. To achieve this fulfillment, there are some concrete things you can do. For example, experiencing success can help you to feel more competent. Organizing your tasks, having an overview of the situation, and bringing your attention to the things that go well can help you increase your fulfillment of the need for competence. Teachers can easily recognize this; when they structure their work better, and help their students to become more focused, it becomes easier to see the desired goals and outcomes of the work. Having clarity in this improves the chance of success. This can lead to better results and feeling more competent. The following activity can help you experience more competence and look at what steps you can take to achieve this.

Being More Successful at Work by Feeling More Competent

Goal: Improving the fulfillment of the need for competence.

Materials: None.

1-1 Choose a (work) situation, for example in teaching or in collaborating with colleagues, in which you didn't feel competent.

Write down:
• What are your actions in a situation like this? How do you feel?
• What signals do you see, or what do you experience that leads you to the conclusion that you are not competent? (Do others see or say this or is this only your own experience?)
• Is this really a problem? Or is it okay to be less competent because you are still learning?

2-2 Exchange. How competent do you feel? Is that really the case or is it only your experience? Is how competent or incompetent you feel a problem for others? If so, in what way? If not, what is the problem?

3-1 There are several things you can do to increase your feeling of competence:
• Formulate concrete goals and small steps forward that are manageable.
• Think about former success experiences in your work or life. Use the positive energy that is brought up by this memory to help you realize that you can be and feel competent.
• Set yourself an achievable goal for your task. Would it be possible, for example, to split this task into five skills or steps that are manageable and which you can learn to master step-by-step?

Write down:
• What is your smaller/manageable goal?
• What small steps can you take and what skills do you need for this?
Step 1...
Step 2...
Step 3...
Step 4...
Step 5...
• Remember a very successful (work) situation. How does this feel? What are you like in this experience? What energy do you feel in this?
• What core qualities are you using?
• Could you use these core qualities in the steps you described just now?

4-2	Exchange. Help each other to describe the manageable steps and how setting smaller goals can help you to experience more success.
5-G	Discuss with the whole group, focusing on manageable goals and experiences of success. What is the benefit for your motivation and self-confidence when you can see manageable goals and experiences of success? What core qualities can support you in this?
6-1	What core qualities can you use to help you take these small steps and to start feeling more confident? (For example: confidence, willpower, enthusiasm.)
7-2	Exchange. What core qualities can you use? Help each other to find relevant core qualities and to feel them. (Note: the latter is something quite different from *thinking* about them; help each other to really *feel* them in the here-and-now.)
9-G	Make and discuss plans for future steps.

34 Becoming More Motivated by Increasing Your Sense of Autonomy

Your feeling of autonomy is increased when you make clear choices, are true to yourself, and hold your vision at times when you feel that you are not being seen. Making sure you are being seen and heard increases your feeling of autonomy. This is not an easy task in education, because if you are a teacher, you don't just have your own autonomy to deal with, but also that of your students. You are a part of a large system that doesn't always give attention to your needs. When it comes to autonomy, teachers often feel split between pressure from management and pressure from students (Pelletier, Séguin-Lévesque, & Legault, 2002).

The following activity can help you to experience fulfillment of autonomy and to explore what you can do yourself to achieve this.

Becoming More Motivated by Increasing Your Sense of Autonomy

Goal: Improving the fulfillment of the need for autonomy.

Materials: None.

1-1 Choose a (work) situation, for example in teaching or in administrative work, in which you didn't feel autonomous.
Write down:
• What is this situation like? What is it that makes you feel not autonomous? How do you feel?
• What signals do you see, or what do you experience that leads you to the conclusion that you are not autonomous?
• What do you want to be autonomous in? What do you want? What is your ideal?

2-2 Exchange. How competent do you feel? Is that really the case, or is it only your experience? In what and how would you like to be more autonomous? Why is this not happening? What is stopping you?

3-1 There are different things you can do to increase your sense of autonomy:
• Consciously reflect on and use your core qualities.
• Revisit earlier experiences of autonomy in your work or life. Use the positive energy of this memory to create a feeling of autonomy now.
Write down:
• What is your ideal, and how do you feel when you do feel autonomous in this situation?
• What core qualities can you use? (For example: compassion, clarity, honesty, vigor, willpower, trust, calmness, being true to yourself, etc.)
• Remember an experience in which you felt very autonomous. How did that feel? What are you like in that experience? What energy do you feel?
• What core qualities are you using?
• Link this feeling to the situation you chose at the beginning of this activity. What is the effect of this?
• Verbalize a concrete intention to be more autonomous (for example: what you do and don't do; how will you be true to yourself in this situation?)

4-2 Exchange. Help each other to find and feel the core qualities that increase a sense of autonomy in this situation.

5-G Discuss with the whole group: What core qualities are supportive?

	6-1	**Write down:** • What core qualities will you start using? • How will you do this? • How will you help yourself to remember this in that situation? • What will that situation look like then? (Write down what you are like when you use those core qualities.)
	7-G	Discussion, focusing on: When does autonomy happen at the expense of others and in what situations does it benefit others when you have an increased sense of autonomy? What conclusions can be drawn from this? Write down your intentions.

35 Improved Contact with Your Students or Colleagues through Increased Relatedness

Having positive contact with people increases your feeling of relatedness. This is also increased when you consciously make contact and use core qualities such as compassion, attention, and care. Teachers will certainly recognize this in their interaction with the students they have positive contact with. However, it is important to learn to do this consciously until it is second nature, as well as in situations in which you tend to feel more negative. This will help you to learn to use more of your potential, and more situations will become fulfilling.

This activity can help you to experience relatedness and to explore what you can do yourself to achieve this.

Improved Contact with Your Students or Colleagues through Increased Relatedness		
Goal: Increasing the fulfillment of the need for relatedness. **Materials:** None.	1-1	Choose a (work) situation, for example in teaching or in collaborating with colleagues, in which you didn't feel competent. **Write down:** • What is this situation like? Who is there? What is it that makes you feel disconnected? • How does this make you feel? • What signals do you see, or what experience leads you to the conclusion that you don't have (positive) contact? (Are others doing or saying something that indicates this?)
	2-2	Exchange. How connected do you feel? Is this really the case, or is it only your experience? Does your feeling of relatedness cause a problem for others? If so, in what way? If not, what is the problem?

3-1	There are several things you can do to increase your sense of relatedness: • Make contact and use core qualities and social skills. • Revisit earlier experiences of relatedness in your work or life. Use the positive energy from these to realize that you can indeed feel connected. **Write down:** • What is your ideal, and how would it feel if you experienced relatedness in this situation? • What core qualities can you use? (For example: compassion, humor, empathy, trust, calmness, etc.) • Remember an experience in which you felt very connected. How did that feel? What are you like in that experience? What energy do you feel? • What core qualities are you using? Link these qualities to the situation you chose at the beginning of this activity. What is that like? • What is your intention now?
4-2	Exchange. Help each other to find and feel the core qualities that increase the sense of relatedness.
5-G	Discussion within the group: What core qualities can support you?
6-1	**Write down:** • What core qualities will you start using? • How will you do this? • How will you help yourself to remember this in that situation? • What will that situation look like then? (Write down what you are like when you use those core qualities.)
7-G	Discuss your reflections, focusing on: When do you benefit from being led by your need for relatedness, and when do you lose your uniqueness by needing to be part of the group? Write down your conclusions and intentions.

36   Exploring Different Types of Ideals

We saw earlier that ideals play a part in experiencing meaning and purpose in life. Ideals are linked with your core qualities and give direction to your development. When your ideals are clear and when you know how to use the right core qualities it is easier to realize your ideals.

There are several types of ideals. For example, there are ideals that really suit you and help you to grow, and there are also ideals that you have as compensation for something you are missing. You can even have ideals that really don't suit you but which you copy from others unconsciously.

The following activity will help you to explore your ideals and increase their power.

Exploring Different Types of Ideals		
Goal: Exploring different types of ideals.	1-1	Put the 'Ideals' cards in front of you. Try to divide them into three groups of ideals. Think of your own names for the three groups. **Write down:** • What are the groups you made? What names did you give each group? • What type of ideal is in each of the groups? • What difference do the ideals in the three groups have in terms of their power?
Materials: 'Ideals' cards (@, pdf #5); possibly 'Core qualities' cards (@, pdf #6); and blank cards.		
	2-4	Compare your groupings. **One of you writes down:** • What groups did you make? • What is the difference between the groups?
	3-G	Discussion within the whole group: Is there a connection between the groups of ideals and the three types of needs (a, b, and c) we discussed at the beginning of this chapter?
	4-1	Choose from each group one ideal that you have yourself or write a similar ideal on a blank card. **Write down:** • What do these ideals mean to you? • How do each of these ideals shape your work or life? • What core qualities are you using to realize these ideals? • How well does this work for you?
	5-2	Exchange. Discuss how an ideal that you have comes through in your work or life. What are you doing to realize this ideal?
	6-G	Discuss with the whole group, focusing on core qualities.

Doing inspiring work	Using my creativity optimally
Ideals 9	Ideals 10
Realizing my deepest dreams	Close friendships
Ideals 11	Ideals 12

Examples of 'Ideals' cards

37 Exploring Your Own Ideals

You often have several ideals at the same time. The following activity helps you discover some of these different ideals in your work and life. They can help to strengthen each other but can also weaken each other if they are opposites.

Therefore, one of the questions is whether your ideals complement each other or whether they actually weaken each other at certain points. Did you really choose these ideals yourself or are they others' expectations of you? The more an ideal is really yours (and connected to your other ideals), the stronger its power.

Exploring Your Own Ideals		
Goal: Exploring different types of ideals in your life; using the elevator; using the power of your ideals. **Materials:** Five blank cards.	1-1	Take five blank cards. Write on each of the blank cards an ideal related to: • Something you would like to have. • Something you would like to be able to do. • A choice you really want to make. • The kind of relationships you would like to have. • Who you want to be in your work.
	2-2	Discuss your ideals. What energy do you get from these ideals?

3-G	Discuss with the whole group: How are the ideals differ-ent? Which ideals are connected with a feeling of useful-ness or meaning in your life? What is the power you get from these ideals?	
4-1	**Write down:** • (How) are these five ideals connected? Or are they opposites? Or are they not related? • (How) do they strengthen each other? • Is it easy to replace these ideals? If so, what are the ideals that are really stable in your life? • Are these ideals related to a sense of meaning in your life?	
5-2	Exchange. Focus on the connection between ideals. Also discuss how ideals are an expression of who you are or of a sense of meaning. Help each other to discover how much power you give to these ideals (or not). Which core qualities help you to realize an ideal?	
6-G	Discuss within the whole group and share ideals.	

38   Using the Power of an Ideal to Complete a Task

When you can link an ideal to your work, education (or professional devel-opment), or concrete tasks, this may result in inner power and a sense of direction. Something can go really well when it truly fits your ideal. But when you do something that is not aligned with your ideal, this can cause problems. In that case, you can look at what you can do to become more in touch with your ideal. You could also look at what core qualities you can use to stay truer to your ideal. Another thing you can do is to look at how you can adjust your task or situation in such a way that it becomes aligned with your ideal. If this is not possible, you could consider changing tasks or look-ing for something else that does suit you. The question is: How can you stay true to what you really want?

Using the Power of an Ideal to Complete a Task

Goal: Using the power of an ideal for a task in the context of your work or professional development. **Materials:** None.	1-1	Choose a task that you have for your work or professional development, for example in teaching a particular lesson or in educational development. **Write down:** • What is this task? What are you doing for this task? What is the goal? • What is your ideal in this task? If you don't have any ideals in this particular case, what could be a relevant ideal you have in general? • How would you benefit from realizing this ideal? • What core qualities can you use to realize this ideal?
	2-2	Exchange. What is your ideal? What core qualities are you using to realize your ideal?
	3-G	Discussion within the group.
	4-1	**Write down:** • What concrete actions will you take to realize your ideal? • What core qualities could you use to make it easier in this case to realize your ideal easily and as well as possible?
	5-2	Exchange and help each other to make concrete plans and to link them to core qualities.
	6-G	Discuss and help each other to clarify and strengthen your intentions.

39 Focusing Your Ideals

When your ideal is really clear to you, it becomes very powerful, and therefore much easier to realize. The following activity is aimed at getting a clear picture of one of your ideals.

Focusing Your Ideals

Goal: Becoming focused by clearly and consciously visualizing ideals. **Materials:** None.	1-1	**Write down:** • What ideal is important to you (for example in your work, professional development, life, etc.)? Describe the ideal situation, and visualize this clearly. • Also, see if there might be another 'deeper' ideal hidden underneath this ideal that has something to do with usefulness or meaning in your life.

2-2	Describe your ideals to each other. Help each other to paint the image of your ideal as clearly as possible. Also check if there is another ideal hidden underneath.
3-G	Discussion within the whole group. Something that might work well is to imagine your ideal as a real-life movie or picture. To do this, imagine yourself in a future where your ideal has been completely realized. Visualize this and fully absorb the image.
4-1	Make a picture, as detailed as possible, of your ideal and connect with the feeling of it. **Write down:** • How is your environment when your ideal has been realized? • What do you see? • What are you doing? • What is it you are good at? • What are your main convictions or beliefs when your ideal has been realized? • What are you like when your ideal has been realized? • What is the deepest meaning this ideal has for you?
5-2	Discuss your experiences. Help each other to clarify the ideal.
6-G	Share with the group.
7-1	**Write down:** • What new insight do you now have about your ideal? • What is one concrete intention you will start working on?

40   Addressing Your Doubts About Ideals

You might have some doubts about your ability to realize your ideals. Ideals are nice, but are they perhaps too idealistic? Will you be able to do it? What might happen to prevent your ideals from coming true? The positive side of these doubts is that you become alert and clear, and you might end up putting more energy into realizing your ideals. The disadvantage could be, however, that your ideal is weakened by your doubts. To remove this limitation, it can help to look consciously at what you are really, unconsciously, doing to limit the power of an ideal. In other words: Are you getting in your own way, and how? Once you are clearer on this you can help yourself to keep faith in your ideal and overcome doubts. It might not be possible to remove these doubts completely, but you can stop them from blocking you.

However, you have to be able to look at them first. This is the theme of the following activity.

Addressing Your Doubts About Ideals		
Goal: Describing and challenging the limiting beliefs regarding realizing your ideals. **Materials:** Yellow and pink sticky notes.	1-1	**Write down:** • An (important) ideal you have regarding your work in education, or an ideal in your professional development (on a yellow note). • Write some clear doubts you have about your ability to realize this ideal (on pink notes). • What do you notice in writing down these doubts? • Could there be a negative belief at the root of them?
	2-2	Exchange, addressing your ideals and doubts. Help each other to organize the doubts (on the pink notes) from strong to weak doubts.
	3-G	Exchange, discussing ideals and types of doubts. What effect do the doubts have?
	4-1	Choose a strong doubt you have about your ability to realize your ideal. **Write down:** • What is the doubt? Why do you have this doubt? • What core qualities do you need to reduce or eliminate this doubt? • Imagine that this doubt has disappeared. How do you feel? What do you think? What do you do? Create a powerful image of yourself with this/these new core quality/qualities, completely clear of the doubt.
	5-2	Help each other with steps 1 to 4 to address the doubt. Use core qualities that might help you. What do you achieve by using these?
	6-G	Share with the group and strengthen the image of using the core qualities.

41 Using Your Inner Resources

Positive experiences can give you strength by showing you what is possible. They also create an emotional buffer, a reservoir you can draw from when you have a setback. They give you resilience. Therefore, we talk about positive experiences as 'resources.' The following activity will help you to start drawing from and using these resources.

Using Your Inner Resources		
Goal: Becoming aware of how positive experiences you've had in the past can act as an inner resource for you to draw from. **Materials:** None.	1-1	Name a problem you have, or something you would like to change. **Write down:** • What is your problem? • What is your ideal? • What do you need (inside) to achieve this ideal?
	2-2	Exchange and discuss what you wrote.
	3-G	Discuss with the group. Also, talk about the power of a positive experience you've had in the past.
	4-1	Remember a successful experience, an experience in which you encountered a (similar) problem and you were able to reach your ideal. (If you find this difficult, you can choose an experience that is more obviously successful.) Now imagine you are re-living this experience. **Write down:** • What power do you feel in this success experience? • What skills help with that? • What core qualities are supporting this? Use the power of these core qualities to have confidence in your abilities (here and now!). • What core qualities are helping you now?
	5-2	Exchange, focusing on the power of the earlier success experience and the confidence that can be gained from that. Help each other to connect with this positive experience.
	6-G	Discuss, and help each other to strengthen the experience of success.

42 Using a Role Model as a Source of Inspiration and Strength

It can be stimulating to see someone who is able to successfully do something you would like to be able to do yourself. The strength of their core qualities can be very inspiring and can help you to pull yourself up to their example. In the following activity we will look at how you can use an inspiring person and their core qualities as a resource.

Using a Role Model as a Source of Inspiration and Strength

Goal: Using a successful role model as a source of inspiration, to tap into your inner power.

Materials: None.

1-1	Remember a situation in which you saw someone do something you would like to be able to do. This could be someone you know directly, for example a teacher from your own school years, or a colleague, a fellow student, someone you have seen on television, etc. Try to choose someone you admire. **Write down:** • What is this person good at? How can you see that? • What skills does this person use? • What core qualities does this person use? How do you experience those? • What can this person do that you would like to be able to do?
2-2	Exchange, focusing on the core quality and energy you get from seeing this inspiring role model.
3-G	Discuss with the group, focusing on activating the core qualities of this role model (here and now!).
4-1	**Write down:** • What are the core qualities that this person applies which you use less or not yet? • If you assume that you also have these core qualities, how could you start to use and strengthen these? • What concrete actions will you take to use these core qualities more?
5-2	Exchange, focusing on core qualities. Spell out a concrete intention. Help each other to make this intention as specific as possible.
6-G	Share with the group, strengthening the intentions and making them more specific.

SCIENTIFIC BACKGROUND

Self-Determination Theory

Since the 1970s, *Self-Determination Theory* (SDT) has taken an important role in the theory of human motivation (Deci & Ryan, 2000, 2002; Ryan & Deci, 2000b, 2002). SDT provides a coherent framework that describes what makes people's psychology healthy, a framework that has many links with other areas of psychology. It assumes three basic psychological needs: the need for competence, autonomy, and relatedness. The fulfillment of these basic psychological needs is connected to intrinsic motivation, experiencing well-being, optimal functioning, self-confidence, engagement, psychological growth, and vitality (Deci & Ryan, 2000, 2002).

When there are external factors that can help to fulfill the three basic psychological needs, this adds extra benefit to the continued psychological growth of the person (Deci & Ryan, 2000, p. 229). Organizations that manage to help their employees to fulfill the three basic needs are often very successful because of it (Deci *et al.*, 2001; Sheldon & Bettencourt, 2002). The effects of suppressing the three basic psychological needs are further discussed in Chapter 6, in the context of dealing with obstacles.

Competence

The meaning of the term 'competence' within SDT is based on the work of White (1959, in Elliot, McGregor, & Trash, 2002, p. 361), who states that organisms are born with the urge to influence and control their environment. The need for competence is not the desire to have concrete skills but the desire to experience confidence in the effectiveness of one's own actions (Ryan & Deci, 2002, p. 7). Experiencing competence, therefore, points to the feeling of being in control, feeling able to use one's capacity, and experiencing this in interacting with the social environment (Deci, 1975; Ryan & Deci, 2002).

Autonomy

Autonomy is the desire to organize your own experiences and behavior, and to perform activities that are in harmony with how you see yourself and congruent with your values and interests (Deci & Ryan, 2000, p. 231; Ryan, Kuhl, & Deci, 1997; Sheldon & Elliot, 1999). Autonomy therefore refers to the need to experience the authentic self ('the core') as the source of one's actions (Ryan, 1995; Ryan & Deci, 2002; Skinner & Edge, 2002, p. 298). Central to experiencing autonomy is the will: making clear choices from your conscious values, and taking responsibility for your own choices and behavior (Hodgins, Koestner, & Duncan, 1996).

SDT emphasizes that the greater one's autonomy, the more the person acts according to his or her own values and intentions. This is counter to reacting to other forces, whether from inside (such as floating passions) or outside (social pressure) (Ryan *et al.*, 1997, p. 702).

According to SDT, autonomous people tend to develop their own sense of initiative and tend to look for interesting and challenging activities (Deci & Ryan, 2000; Ryan & Deci, 2001; Sheldon & Houser-Marko, 2001). Teachers who feel autonomous seem to be better at supporting autonomy in their students, whereas teachers who are not autonomous seem to be more in need of control (Pelletier *et al.*, 2002).

Relatedness

The need for relatedness indicates a desire to experience positive relationships and feel connected to others. Relatedness has to do with caring for others, the feeling that other people care about you and that you are part of a community or a group (Baumeister & Leary, 1995; Ryan, 1995; Ryan & Deci, 2002). The need for relatedness becomes fulfilled as people are experienced more as trustworthy, supportive, friendly, and sage, and as relationships become more durable and lasting (Epstein, 1998a, 1998b; Ryan, Sheldon, Kasser, & Deci, 1996, p. 17). Another expression of this need is the desire for reciprocal, deep, loving, and affectionate relationships.

The Relations between the Three Basic Needs

It seems that the three basic needs are not opposites of each other but, rather, strengthen each other. Conversely, it also seems that when one of the basic needs is suppressed, the fulfillment of the others is also reduced (Deci & Ryan, 2002).

Ideals and Goals in Your Life

Sheldon (2002) proposes that goals and ideals corresponding with your need for autonomy form an important positive power in your life (see also Sheldon & Houser-Marko, 2001). However, people can also have goals and ideals in their life that they have (often unconsciously) taken on from their environment (Sheldon, 2002; Peterson & Seligman, 2004, p. 255).

In that case, people are directed and even conditioned by external factors. For people who are strongly led by their environment, it seems that rewards, deadlines, and instructions from others determine the direction they are going in. They focus more on what others want than on their own ideals. This can certainly give a superficial sense of fulfillment, but does not give a direct and essential fulfillment of the basic psychological needs (Deci & Ryan, 2002).

5 Going With the Flow

While teaching today, John felt that everything seemed to fall perfectly into place. It was effortless; complicated things seemed to happen spontaneously, and the students were so motivated that they continued their team work even after the class. Time flew by and it seemed like everything happened naturally. John had a fantastic day with his students; everything was in flow.

43 Introductory Activity: Recognizing Flow

We will first look for an example of flow in your work or personal experiences.

Introductory Activity: Recognizing Flow		
Goal: Recognizing flow in a situation.	1-1	Remember a positive experience in which you were in full action, in which you were completely absorbed, and everything seemed to happen spontaneously.
Materials: None.	2-1	Recall yourself in this situation. What are you doing? What are you capable of? Are you being challenged or 'sucked in' somehow? How do you feel?

Probably you have experienced flow at some point in your life. When you are in flow, you seem to lose yourself and become absorbed in what you are doing. Everything seems to happen perfectly. It seems like things happen automatically. It gives you energy, more than you are putting in. It all seems to happen without thinking, even though you are doing a lot, and are consciously present. Csikszentmihalyi (1990, 1997) distinguishes the various characteristics of flow (see Table 5.1).

Flow is a natural potential of people. People work and live optimally when they are in flow. Experiences of flow are often the most inspiring and valuable moments in your life. Flow happens when you feel that the things you do are working and that you are good at them.

But all of this is not really enough to reach flow, because when you are very good at doing something, you often strive to be better at it and want to be challenged more. When your skills and level of challenge are in balance,

Characteristics	Example
Concrete goals and immediate feedback on your actions.	Usually there is a clear goal in your actions and you experience immediately if you are getting a result. Hence, you know whether to continue with your action.
Balance between the level of challenge and your personal skills.	You want to achieve something that is actually possible. It is almost like a game to reach the end goal of the challenge.
Blending of action and awareness.	You are completely absorbed in your action. You even forget that you are doing something. It happens automatically.
Extreme concentration and focus.	Your attention is completely focused on the action. You are completely absorbed by it.
Feeling in control.	It is all happening, going well and you have a sense of control over your actions.
'Losing yourself'.	When you are in flow you lose, even if for a brief moment, your sense of self, and don't experience thinking, feeling, and wanting. Your self-consciousness dissolves. Afterwards you 'wake up' and realize what happened.
Different sense of time.	When you are in flow you lose your sense of time. One minute may seem to take an hour, or the hours fly by and feel like a few minutes.
Autotelic experience: Action has its intrinsic value.	Action and the reason, or end-goal of the action, dissolve into each other. Action is for its own sake. The doing has become the goal.

Table 5.1   Characteristics of flow

this enables flow. You are at the edge of your ability, but you notice that you are successful (Figure 5.1).

One example might be that you can play the piano fairly well, but you would really like to be able to play along with a piece of music from your favorite CD. This doesn't seem so easy at first. You listen, figure out the notes you have to play and suddenly notice that you can play along really well and that it sounds good. This gives you the opportunity to be in flow.

Flow can also work in groups, even when you are a teacher in a class that is difficult to work with. However difficult it normally is, sometimes you can have one of those days where everything works; you are able to smoothly do the things that are usually difficult, the students are motivated, you are motivated, and suddenly everything happens by itself. You and the class are in mutual flow; the flow seems contagious. It is a fantastic experience.

However, when you are very good at something, but you are not being challenged enough or at all, it is possible to get bored after a while. For

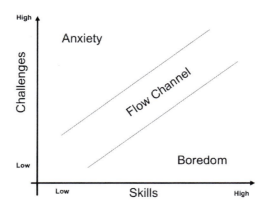

Figure 5.1   The flow model (adapted from Csikszentmihalyi, 1990)

example, it might be very easy for you to create cooperative exercises for the students. You master the necessary insights and skills, the students enjoy everything, and it all runs smoothly. If there is no new challenge, it might all become a boring routine. It starts to get fun again when something new and challenging appears. For example, a new project in which group work is linked to an international visit or exchange program with another school, something you have never done before. Now there is a chance that you can experience flow again in your work.

However, the challenge can also be too big. When you are not so skilled at doing something and you are challenged a lot, you could become scared and unable to do it. For example, you might be quite good at making plans for your school and writing policies. But the moment your school principal asks you as an 'expert' to give a lecture to a room of 150 educational experts and school principals, this might be too much. This can make you feel fearful and stressed. The challenge could be too big for you. You might feel like giving up.

44   Introductory Activity: Increasing Flow; Work as Play

Flow appears when there is a positive challenge. You can see this really well in young children. They are virtually in permanent flow, and the moment they are not, you notice immediately. They start to moan or become ill. For example, children will only start to walk when they are ready for it, and then they can be completely absorbed in it. They are fully 'in the moment.' They are constantly balancing on the edge of being able to do something and being challenged to do more. Play is the driver of their flow; they lose themselves in play and through play, they explore themselves, others, and the world.

As an adult we often limit our flow in all sorts of ways. We believe that flow can only occur occasionally, which results in us making things more and more complicated. Then we experience a problem and we make it even more difficult for ourselves when we try to analyze the problem inside ourselves. We end up trying to use our analytical mind, while the flow is actually still inside us. It is the basic ability to be who you really are.

What counts for young children and students also applies to adults. Adults, too, learn more easily in play and have a more joyful experience through that. This is also called *'playfulness.'* Playfulness creates a feeling of flow very easily. Therefore, an open, spontaneous, and playful attitude to life and work can be a powerful way to create flow in your life. The following activity will help you to explore the connections between playful situations and experiencing flow. It will also help you to explore how to bring play into your work and life, and through doing this, increase flow.

Introductory Activity: Increasing Flow; Work as Play		
Goal: Recognizing the connection between play and flow.	1-1	Recall a game that you used to play as a child that you became completely absorbed in. **Write down:** What was the game? How did it feel to play it?
Materials: None.	2-1	Recall a fun, challenging activity you used to do with others. **Write down:** What activity was this? What did this challenge feel like?
	3-1	Remember a (work) experience in which there was inventiveness, creativity, originality, humor, and joy. **Write down:** What was this situation like? What did you feel in this situation?
	4-1	Remember a challenging (work/learning) situation with a positive element of competition that felt like a match or game. **Write down:** What was this situation? What did this element of competition or play feel like?
	5-1	Describe whether and how this type of play corresponds with the experience of flow in your work or life in general (see Table 5.1). Think of something you could do in the next couple of weeks to use the power of this playful attitude in a task or at work.

FURTHER EXPLORATION

What is the secret of flow? How do you experience flow in your life? Are there different levels of flow? What is it like when there is no flow? The following activities are focused on finding answers to questions like these. The insights you gain from this can help you to create flow more consciously, and to use its positive elements more effectively.

45   Exploring Flow and Non-flow

In Figure 5.2, you can see a more detailed model than in Figure 5.1. This model also gives gradations of flow and non-flow, depicted in feeling-words. The horizontal axis shows how skilled you feel. The further to the right, the higher your sense of success in what you do. The vertical axis shows the level of challenge. The higher you are on this vertical line, the more you are feeling challenged. Experiencing flow is all about the balance of feeling skillful and challenged. This is depicted in the area in the top-right of the diagram; the challenge is high, but you feel very skillful. Then you are in the flow area.

When you feel unchallenged and not skilled you are more to the bottom left of the diagram. Sometimes this happens when you just sit in front of the

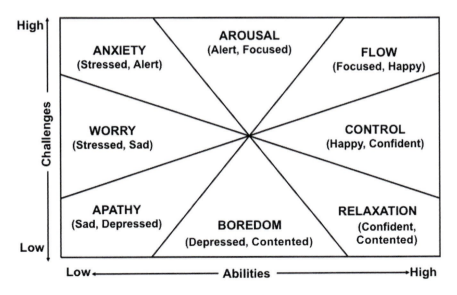

Figure 5.2   The elaborate flow model (Csikszentmihalyi, 1997)

television, when you are hanging around on the sofa and not a lot is happening. When the challenge is high and you don't feel very skilled, there is the chance you will feel stressed, in which case you are in the section 'worry' or even 'anxiety.' When you have a reasonable sense of competence but don't feel challenged, you will get bored etc. (See the different sections and terms in Figure 5.2.) In the following activity we will explore this flow model further, through the question of how flow works for you in your work and life. What more could you do to create flow in your work or life?

Exploring Flow and Non-flow		
Goal: Becoming aware of what creates flow and non-flow; observing how you get more flow in your own work and life.	1-1	Have a look at the elaborate flow model (Figure 5.2). **Write down:** • What are three concrete experiences you have had recently, in which you felt: (a) worried; (b) bored; and (c) in flow. • Describe for each of these three experiences how strongly you felt: (a) challenged; and (b) competent.
Materials: Elaborate flow model (Figure 5.2; see @, pdf #20).	2-2	Exchange. What do you notice in terms of your feeling of competence and challenge in these three experiences?
	3-G	Discuss with the group, focusing on the feeling of competence and the challenge of the experience. Is it possible to align your feeling of competence and the challenges you take on? If so, how?
	4-1	**Write down:** • What does flow mean for you? • How important is flow for you? • Can you consciously align your feeling of competence and the challenges you take on? • How could you do this in a difficult situation? • How could you do this in a stressful situation?
	5-2	Exchange. What lessons can you learn from these reflections?
	6-G	Exchange, focusing on how you can experience more flow.
	7-1	**Write down:** What will you do in the coming weeks to experience more flow?

46 Using Core Qualities to Increase Flow

What core qualities help you get into flow? Sometimes it could be 'precision,' at other times 'courage,' and yet at other times it is vigor, idealism, creativity, or care. Or could it be inner peace, trust, or determination? When you are in flow you usually use your core qualities unconsciously. Would it be possible to increase flow by *consciously* using them?

When you see flow as a stream, you could look at how using your core qualities can activate the source of this stream. In other words, is it possible to invoke the experience of flow by using core qualities, even at times when there is no flow at all?

Using Core Qualities to Increase Flow
This activity is a continuation of Activity 45.

Goal: Investigating the connection between using a core quality and developing flow.

Materials: 'Core qualities' cards (@, pdf #6).

1-1 Remember a personal flow experience (one you had while you were on your own).
Write down:
• Why was this a flow experience?
• What core quality/qualities did you use in this experience? (You can select core qualities from the cards.)
Now go back in your memory to a flow experience in a group (one you had with others).
Write down:
• Why was this a flow experience?
• What core quality/qualities did you use in this experience?

2-2 **Discuss:**
Which two experiences did you choose? Why?
What core qualities did you use in each of the situations? Is there a difference between the core qualities? If so, what is it that makes this difference?

3-G Discuss with the group, focusing on:
• What core qualities do you use in a flow experience?
• What is the difference between flow as an individual experience and flow in a group?
Also discuss the thought of using core qualities consciously to create (more) flow.

4-1	Now choose three core qualities that are easy to use. **Write down:** • What are the core qualities? • To what extent does calling on each of these core qualities invoke a feeling of flow (or the beginning of flow)? • To what extent are you dependent on your environment in this? Now choose three core qualities you use less often but that are nonetheless important for your work (for example: precision, persistence, involvement, perspective). **Write down:** • What core qualities did you choose? • How can using each of these three core qualities help you to get (more) into a flow zone?
5-2	Exchange and compare the two groups of core qualities. Help each other to clearly spell out how you can get more into the flow by using core qualities.
6-G	Exchange the main insights you developed in step 5-2 and think about concrete applications. Discuss to what extent using core qualities can help you to get (more) into a flow zone.
7-1	**Write down:** • What core qualities can you use in an upcoming (work) situation to help you experience more flow? • How will you do that?

Some people find the idea of creating their own flow tiring. However, the opposite is true: You get tired from apathy and boredom, while flow brings you energy. People may think that they have to constantly work hard to get into flow. Even that is not true, because if you were to put yourself under pressure, it would actually block the flow. It is really all very simple. As an example, look at young children. Unfortunately, though, as adults we may have somewhat lost this natural simplicity in our lives.

47 Increasing the Flow of a Group: Flow is Contagious

When you are with someone who is bored or apathetic, this can often pass on to you. It will make it more difficult to get into flow. If, however, you are in contact with someone who is in flow, this often has a positive influence.

In short, flow is contagious, but non-flow is also contagious. This is an important principle in education. Think for example about a class of students who are hanging around being bored. In this situation it is more difficult for you to maintain flow. The other way around is true, too: you also affect your students. When a student or a group of students is in flow during the class, this can catch on with other students and you as the teacher. In this case the flow of one or more people has a positive effect on the whole group. Teachers can infect others with their flow and likewise students can bring teachers into flow by being in flow themselves (Bakker, 2005). The effect is that education does not just become more pleasant, but also more effective and better. This can help you to re-think your own role in professional interactions.

The following activity will help you to look at the phenomenon of group flow and show you options to help create group flow.

Increasing the Flow of a Group: Flow is Contagious

Goal: Recognizing group flow; discovering how you can promote group flow.

Materials: Optional: elaborate flow model (Figure 5.2, pdf #20) and 'Core qualities' cards (@, pdf #6).

1-1 Take a look at situations you have experienced in a group in which you think there was group flow (e.g. during a class, sport, music, discussion, theatre, etc.)
Write down:
• What are examples of group flow you have experienced? (Assign a key word to each of them.)
• For each example: What do you think was the reason for the flow? Pay attention to the feeling of competence and challenge (use the flow model in Figure 5.2).
• Was there a common goal in these examples?
• Was there joy?

2-2 Exchange. Have you had the experience of group flow? What are the characteristics of group flow? How is group flow created?

3-G Discussion: Focus on finding a 'definition' of group flow. How is it created? (Pay attention to the collective experience of competition and challenge.)
What is it exactly that makes flow so contagious?

4-1 **Write down:**
• Name a group you work with a lot.
• What can you do in this group to stimulate flow?
• What core qualities can help you with this? (You can use the core quality cards for this if necessary.)

5-4	Exchange and determine what you can do as an individual to promote group flow. Is there a correlation with using a core quality? Write down your findings on a sheet of paper.
6-G	Share the findings of your team. Focus on what it was that helped to promote the flow of the group. What are the relationships between group flow and using core qualities?
7-1	**Write down:** • What core qualities will you start to use in the near future in a group to promote flow? • How will you decide whether it is successful?

SCIENTIFIC BACKGROUND

Experiences of flow bring positive energy. According to Csikszentmihalyi (1990, 1997), flow is the experience of being absorbed in an activity in which self-consciousness disappears, and action has a value in itself. As we indicated earlier in this chapter, flow can be created by:

- clear goals and instant feedback on actions;
- a balance between the level of challenge and personal skills;
- blending of actions and awareness;
- powerful concentration and focus;
- a feeling of control.

Ryan and Deci (2000a) describe flow as a phenomenon that is connected to the fulfillment of the three basic psychological needs (the need for competence, autonomy, and relatedness; see Chapter 4). According to these authors, the concept of flow can be improved by seeing the fulfillment of these three basic needs as a central characteristic of it. (This is not how it is seen at the moment; flow is seen more as an ultimate experience of competence.)

Ryan and Deci's line of thinking is quite understandable since the feeling of being able to do something really well and being challenged in it, is closely connected to the fulfillment of the need for competence. If the need for relatedness is also fulfilled, for example, in team work when you feel one with the team, flow is further increased. And if, on top of this, you also feel autonomous (you choose the challenge and it fits completely with what you want) this makes the flow even more intense. In this situation you are in touch with who you really are inside, your deepest sense of "this is who I am," your core. If you experience this a lot in your life, you will express more and more who you feel you are. You will start to use your full potential and 'live' the qualities of your core. In Chapter 1, we mentioned this as being called *self-actualization* (Hodgins & Knee, 2002). Csikszentmihalyi (1993) also speaks about *transcenders* when he references people who have many flow experiences and who use core qualities such as humanity, solidarity, and social intelligence. Transcenders transcend self-interests.

Flow is contagious (Bakker, 2005). This means that people can 'infect' each other and achieve group flow (Marotto, Roos, & Victor, 2007). In addition, the element of play is important in flow (Chen, Yen, Hung, & Huang, 2008).

6 Letting Go of Limitations

Simon is not feeling comfortable in meetings with his colleague teachers. He feels insecure and thinks to himself, "There is nothing of value for me to add." This thought makes him tense and as a result, when someone asks him something in the meeting, he starts to stutter and flounder. And he thinks, "You see, I am worthless . . ." This is why he usually tries to stay in the background during meetings.

People keep running into problems, in their work or in their private life. They can be small or large. And they make people less happy than they would like to be. Life just doesn't quite flow right. In the previous chapters we took a look at what can be done about this. It is also a good idea to investigate the factors inside of us that can block flow. By looking at these factors we can learn to remove those blocks at their root.

It is quite striking that people have certain ways in which they block their own potential for flow, for example, through self-destructive thoughts or beliefs. They often become a kind of default setting in the way one relates to oneself. Since these negative patterns block one's flow and optimal functioning, we call them obstacles. One common obstacle people often create is putting themselves under pressure ("I must . . ."). Another is negative thinking ("I wouldn't be able to do that anyway," "I am not interesting," etc.). You can sometimes see that people are completely led by such unconscious and limiting beliefs. These beliefs have become a leading factor in their lives. This leads to the same situations being repeated again and again. For example, if you often think, "I will not be able to do that anyway" it is possible for this idea to develop into a powerful belief: "I am a failure." This belief is, of course, a logical reaction (to yourself) to problems you have experienced in your life, but as a result you will experience less and less success. You will start to assume in advance that all sorts of things will go wrong again, and this will negatively affect how you cope with situations. We are speaking of a 'self-fulfilling prophesy.'

48 Introductory Activity: Becoming Aware of Your Limiting Thoughts

Limiting thoughts and beliefs can easily surface in difficult situations, even without you noticing. The following activity will help you to look at a few limiting thoughts. You might even recognize a few of your own limiting thoughts.

Introductory Activity: Becoming Aware of Your Limiting Thoughts	

Goal: Become aware of limiting thoughts. **Materials:** None.	1-1	Below we have listed a few limiting thoughts. Look at each of them. • I am a bit odd! • I can't do anything! • You can't trust people! • I am not loved! • I do not matter! • I can't contribute anything valuable! • My life is useless!
	2-1	Choose three you recognize for yourself or someone else. **Write down:** • How does someone feel (e.g. yourself) when they really believe in a belief like this? • How does such a belief influence behavior? • Why would these be called 'limiting beliefs'? • Is it possible to 'let go' of such limiting beliefs?
	3-1	Now take a look at the following seven positive beliefs. They stem from a positive connection to your core. • I am a valuable person! • I can really do what I want! • You can trust people! • People like me! • I add something important by being who I am! • I am inspiring! • My life is purposeful! **Write down:** • What feeling do these seven positive beliefs evoke in you if you really believe in them? (If you are in doubt, what is limiting your trust? Can you let go of this limitation?) • How does a positive belief affect your work and life? • Why would these be called 'supporting beliefs'? • What is the difference between the two lists of beliefs? • What helps you to let go of limiting thoughts and allow more positive beliefs inside yourself?

External and internal limitations

Figure 6.1 shows what happens when our flow is blocked. This image is a variant on Figure 2.1. Compare the two.

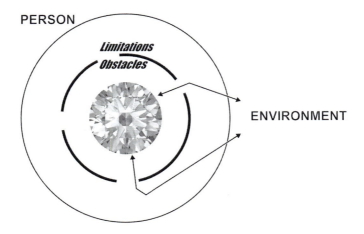

Figure 6.1   The power of core qualities is sometimes limited by internal obstacles

In Figure 2.1 you could see a free flow of energy between the person and their environment. In Figure 6.1 we see that the expression of the core qualities is being restrained. In this image we see that in a situation like this it is possible for some energy to come out, but there is no strong energy coming in and going out. That is what the arrows in Figure 6.1 indicate. The result is that the core qualities of the person only have a weak influence on their environment, and also that this person is now less able to experience their environment the way it really is.

When we run into obstacles at work or in our life, we have a habit of thinking in the first instance that it is an obstacle in our environment. In other words, we tend to think that there are *external obstacles* hindering us, for example, a difficult class or group of students, a difficult colleague, a school that is not inspiring, etc. But Figure 6.1 shows that the obstacle is often inside ourselves (an *internal obstacle*). For example, when we have to interact with a difficult student, this seems obviously a serious external obstacle. But when we focus on this too much and believe that the task can never be fulfilled, we become a serious hindrance to ourselves. This phenomenon occurs regularly. For example, we start to think negatively about our own possibility of achieving something. It is not difficult to see how this can start to seriously limit you. This, in turn, increases the probability that things go wrong, and in the end you say, "I told you so!" The circle is complete: we have brought about what we believed in, which is that we would fail. This is called *a self-fulfilling prophecy*. See also the example at the beginning of the chapter.

This phenomenon is crucial in student learning and may explain much of what goes wrong in a learning process. When faced with a challenge (for example a math test), students often think, "I can never do this." It is not hard to see how this limits their optimal functioning, and when the result is that they fail the test, they think, "You see, I knew it!" This is why the subject of this chapter is also important for supporting learners.

49   Introductory Activity: Recognizing the Self-fulfilling Prophecy

In this activity you can explore how self-fulfilling beliefs play a role for you. It will also help you become aware of the effect these beliefs have on what happens in your life.

Introductory Activity: Recognizing the Self-fulfilling Prophecy		
Goal: Recognizing the role of self-fulfilling beliefs. **Materials:** None.	1-1	Think back to a difficult challenge in your life, a situation in which you were certain it would be successful. What you expected also came true. It was fantastic! **Write down:** • What was the challenge? • What did you feel when you thought about this challenge? • What result did you expect? And what feeling did this give you? • What made the result so positive? What was the reason?
	2-1	Think back to a difficult challenge in your life, about which you felt and expected it would NOT be successful. And what you expected also came true. Everything went wrong! **Write down:** • What was the challenge? • What did you feel when you thought about this challenge? • What result did you expect? And what feeling did this give you? • What made the result so negative? What was the reason?

3-1 Can you also recall a situation in your life in which:
A: you had a very positive expectation, but (by your own doing) it all went wrong?
B: you had a negative expectation and (by your own doing) it ended better?
Now focus on the role of your (positive or negative) expectations. What could you say about these in situations A and B?

4-1 When you compare all the previous situations, is there something you discover about the role of positive and negative expectations in your life?

Write down:
• How do your expectations affect your thoughts?
• How do your expectations affect your feelings?
• How do your expectations affect your motivation?
• How do your expectations affect your actions?
• What concrete steps can you take to make better use of the power of realistic and positive expectations?

FURTHER EXPLORATION

When people encounter problems they usually follow three types of 'survival patterns': fight, flight, or freeze. One person might choose (consciously or unconsciously) to fight, while someone else chooses to flee, and a third to freeze. Sometimes you can see a combination of patterns (for example fighting for a short period, but giving up quickly and deciding on flight). These patterns are often acquired at a young age and sometimes become automatisms. They are certainly understandable defense mechanisms, which can be very useful. However, when they come to dominate your behavior to the extent that you lose control, this has negative consequences for you in the long run. We will now take a closer look at these three survival mechanisms.

50   Becoming Aware of the Fight Response

Situations that put you under pressure can invoke an attitude of anger and fighting. You brace yourself and try to actively change the situation to your advantage. Sometimes you don't notice this habit; it happens more or less unconsciously and automatically. Sometimes this is good and gives you energy, but sometimes it doesn't. Anger can bring you energy but can often also cost energy. When you are angry about something for a long time, it often takes more than it gives. Would it be possible for you, in that situation, to respond strongly without losing energy? For example, a very noisy class makes teachers brace themselves, making them more controlling and strict than they would be with a more flexible and accommodating class. The question is whether this attitude makes best use of the potential and initiative of the class or whether it takes away the flow.

The following activity will help you look at situations in which you tend to react angrily and fight. We'll look at questions such as: How are these situations expressed in my work or life? What does a fighting attitude mean? How does it come about? What do I gain by responding in that way? Are there other options that can be more beneficial?

Becoming Aware of the Fight Response

Goal: Becoming aware of responding by fighting, and the emotions that are connected with that.

Materials: 'Body' picture cards (@, pdf #8).

1-1 Remember a situation in which you felt angry and started to fight.
Take a card with the image of the body:
Make a small drawing on one of the 'Body' picture cards: How did you respond?
Write down:
• How did you feel in this situation? What caused this?
• What is it that brings up your tendency to fight (or defend yourself) in a situation like this?
• Does this tendency occur regularly?
• What do you gain from fighting?
• Overall, are you satisfied with this?

2-2 Exchange. What did you draw? What type of answers did you give? What did you learn?

3-G Discuss with the group. Focus on the why and how of fight responses. What is at stake? What are you trying to achieve or ensure by responding in this way?

4-1 **Write down:**
What core qualities are not being used at that moment that could be applied to help you to cope better with the situation?

5-2 Exchange, with attention on core qualities.

6-G Discuss with the group. Focus on core qualities that can add something positive to the response.

7-1	**Write down:**
	What can you do in a situation like this to let go of your standard reactions and consciously apply those core qualities?
8-2	Exchange.
9-G	Discuss your reflections and spell out your intentions.

51   Becoming Aware of the Flight Response

Situations you find difficult can bring up a tendency to remove yourself from the situation, to flee. Sometimes you don't even notice this reaction yourself, it happens automatically. Sometimes you gain something by fleeing, for example self-preservation and safety, but often not. In that case it becomes more of an unconscious withdrawal, even though it might have been better to stand up for who you are. In these situations, a tendency to flee leads to a feeling of failure, which often brings up negative thoughts about yourself. In the following activity we will look at situations that invoke your tendency to flee. This can be, for example, in a class that seems threatening, in which students make negative comments to each other, and there is no feeling of connection. In such a case, teachers, especially beginners, have a tendency to switch off emotionally and retreat. What is it that brings up this tendency, what do you experience, and how can you cope with this situation differently?

Becoming Aware of the Flight Response

Goal: Becoming aware of the flight response and associated feelings. **Materials:** 'Body' picture cards (@, pdf #8).	1-1	Remember a situation that you experienced as difficult or annoying which gave you the urge to leave. **Take a card:** Make a small drawing on the card of how you responded. **Write down:** • How did you feel in this situation? What was the cause of that feeling? • What is it that brings up your tendency to flee in a situation like this? • Does this tendency occur regularly? • What do you gain from fleeing? • Overall, are you satisfied with this?

2-2	Exchange experiences. What did you draw? What type of answers did you give? What did you learn?	
3-G	Discuss your reflections with the group. Focus on the why and how of flight responses. What is at stake? What are you trying to achieve or insure by responding in this way?	
4-1	**Write down:** What core qualities are not being used at that moment that could be applied to help you to cope better with the situation?	
5-2	Exchange, with attention on core qualities.	
6-G	Discuss your reflections with the group. Focus on core qualities that can add something positive to the response.	
7-1	**Write down:** What can you do in a situation like this to let go of your standard reactions and consciously use those core qualities?	
8-2	Exchange.	
9-G	Discuss your reflections and spell out your intentions.	

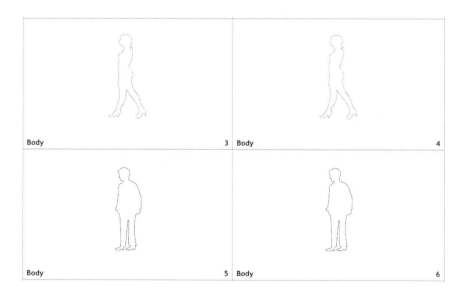

Example of 'Body' picture cards

52 Becoming Aware of Freezing

Situations you find difficult can invoke a sense of not knowing what to do anymore, and lead to you becoming rigid or freezing. The following activity will help you to look at situations that invoke this tendency to freeze. What is it that causes this tendency, what do you experience in that moment, and how can you cope with the situation differently?

Becoming Aware of Freezing		
Goal: Becoming aware of freeze responses. **Materials:** 'Body' picture cards (@, pdf #8).	1-1	Remember a situation that you experienced as difficult or annoying, and in which you had the tendency to freeze. **Take a card:** Make a small drawing of how you responded. **Write down:** • How did you feel in this situation? What was the cause of that? • What is it that brings up your tendency to freeze in a situation like this? • Does this tendency occur regularly? • What do you gain from freezing? • Overall, are you satisfied with this?
	2-2	Exchange experiences. What did you draw? What type of answers did you give? What did you learn?
	3-G	Discuss your reflections with the group. Focus on the why and how of freeze responses. What is at stake? What are you trying to achieve or ensure by responding in this way?
	4-1	**Write down:** What core qualities are not being used at that moment that could be applied to help you cope better with the situation?
	5-2	Exchange, with attention on core qualities.
	6-G	Discuss your reflections with the group. Focus on core qualities that can add something positive to the response.
	7-1	**Write down:** What can you do in a situation like this to let go of your standard reactions and consciously use those core qualities?
	8-2	Exchange.
	9-G	Discuss your reflections and spell out your intentions.

In summary, we can say the following: It can sometimes be very useful to fight, flight, or freeze. If, for example, you are confronted with danger, flight can be a good response. But sometimes this reaction is a habit that is not effective in all situations. The previous activities might have shown you that you often automatically adopt a flight, fight, or freeze pattern, and that it might be possible to retain some flow in particular situations. Consciously applying suitable core qualities can help you with this.

SCIENTIFIC BACKGROUND

Limiting Patterns

When basic psychological needs are not fulfilled, this creates a feeling of being out of control and in danger (Armfield, 2006). According to Epstein (1998a), this can create a range of negative self-images, destructive beliefs, and thoughts, and ineffective behavioral patterns, often without the person being conscious of it. This leads to patterns that can be characterized as fight, flight, and freeze (Skinner & Edge, 2002; Bracha, 2004). People often adopt these patterns in early life and they usually become unconscious habits (Corr, 2010). They are all quite understandable protection mechanisms (Confer *et al.*, 2010) that can certainly be useful, but they can start to dominate people's behavior to the extent that they are not in control of it anymore. In the long term this will have negative consequences for this person and for others (Fredrickson, 2001).

Beliefs

Negative beliefs easily arise in difficult situations, even without the person always being aware of it (Epstein, 1998b). An important effect of negative beliefs is that they reduce the ability to perceive the environment and they limit the ability to interact with it effectively (Fredrickson, 2001). For example, when you believe that the world is dangerous, you see threats everywhere and you may respond by fighting or fleeing. Negative beliefs increase the chance of a negative result and even reinforce themselves (Shani, Tykocinski, Zeelenberg, 2008). However, a positive belief often creates a positive outcome, as was shown through research by Cipriani and Makris (2006).

Internal and External Limitations

People often (unconsciously) blame the causes for negative feelings, experiences, and response patterns on factors outside of themselves. This is called *external attribution* (Boyer, 2006; Fiske & Taylor, 1991). The term 'attribution' stands for the way to explain experiences, in particular successes and failures, with the aim of obtaining an overview of yourself, situations, and your life (Fiske & Taylor, 1991, p. 23). This can lead to developing beliefs about yourself and others, about situations, and even about the world and humanity as a whole (Epstein, 1998b). When these beliefs are negative, they can become limiting. The person can come to think that the limiting factor is in the surroundings, while it should really be attributed to an internal factor.

Autonomous people have less external attributions and look at themselves as the cause of choices and response patterns; they feel responsible for their reactions (Epstein, 1998b; Deci & Ryan, 2002; Weinstein, Brown, & Ryan, 2009).

7 Connecting the Aspects of Your Personality

> Edith is the head of a school department. When you come to her as a student or colleague you feel that she really listens to what you are saying and that she is really trying to support you. She is involved and enthusiastic, and comes up with inspiring suggestions and ideas. Her work vision is that you work together in shaping education. Whenever you talk to Edith, you come away with new ideas and she uses her insight, knowledge, and experience to find a solution that truly opens up new possibilities. You really enjoy meeting her.

The image of a person as we showed it in Figure 2.1 and 6.1 (with a core and inner obstacles around that core), is actually not quite accurate. In reality people are, of course, a lot more complex. People have many different aspects that are not part of their core, but instead are learned (certain habits, worldviews, a self-image, etc.).

In the last few chapters, for example, you might have discovered that, over time, you have developed a tendency to fight. You might even have started to believe that you are a fighter and therefore think that this will always show in everything you do. In this case there is a mix of learned behavior and beliefs, especially beliefs about yourself (your self-image). Aspects such as behavior, beliefs, and self-image determine how you express yourself and how others experience you. In other words, they determine your *personality*. In this chapter we will have a closer look at the meaning of this concept, and see whether we can observe 'layers' within it.

53 Introductory Activity: Recognizing Different Aspects of Your Personality

When you observe yourself you can discover different aspects of your personality. Each one of these says something about you and your relationship with your environment. Together, all these aspects give an overall picture of who you are. It is important to be aware of this in your work or during your training, because an imbalance in this overall picture can have a negative effect on you. In the following activity you will take a look at this.

Introductory Activity: Recognizing Different Aspects of Your Personality

Goal: Exploring the different layers of personality; learning about the onion model.

Materials: None.

1-1 Remember a positive (work) experience and imagine that you are in it again now.

2-1 **Write down:**
• What environment are you in? (Think about the space you are in, the people you are with etc.). What influence does your environment have on your experience?
• What are you doing in this situation?
• Does this show something you are skilled at?
• What key beliefs are guiding you in this situation?
• How do you see yourself and especially your own (professional) role in this situation?
• Do you have a good feeling of "Yes, this is what I'm doing it for!", or do you feel inspired in a different way?

3-1 You have answered six questions that represent six ways of looking at your situation, providing six perspectives. Have a look if you can see an alignment between these six perspectives. Or are they misaligned?

We can interpret these six perspectives as 'layers' of your personality. We do this through the *onion model* (Figure 7.1).

We will now illustrate the six layers of the model and also look at the center of the model: the core.

The onion model

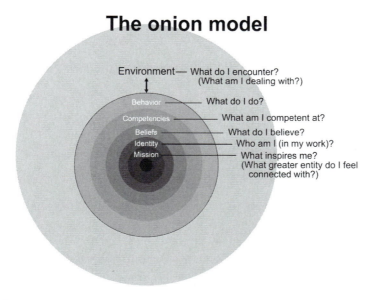

Figure 7.1 The onion model

Layer 1: The environment

This layer is all about the situations you encounter; the problems you are faced with, other people, but also everything that has to do with the wider environment, such as the city or town in which you work or live, or the whole of society. The core question in this layer is: *What do you encounter* (in your environment)?

Layer 2: Behavior

In interacting with your environment, you behave in a certain way. That is the layer of behavior, where the core question is: *What do you do?* It is clear that the first two layers have a mutual effect on each other. The environment affects your behavior and your behavior affects your environment. We will also be able to observe this mutual effect in the following layers.

Layer 3: Competencies

What you do is affected by your competencies (or skills): this is the third layer. This also works the other way around: your behavior influences your competencies. For example, when you notice that you are not able to show a certain behavior that you need in a situation, this can lead to the desire to expand your competencies. The core question is: *What are you competent at?*

Layer 4: Beliefs

This layer is about the vision that is at the root of your competencies and behavior in concrete situations, truths you believe in when interacting with others. With the word 'belief,' we don't mean a religious belief; those belong to layer 6. Examples of this fourth layer are, for example, the beliefs that you can trust the people you are encountering in the situation (e.g. students), or that the task you have to do is similar to one you have completed successfully before. The core question in this layer is: *What do you believe in* (in the situation)?

When someone is continually unable to master something, we sometimes forget to see that this can be caused by underlying beliefs. A student who believes that mathematics is difficult will struggle more with developing his or her mathematical competencies than the student who believes that it is not difficult. The reverse is also true: when you develop certain competencies, you can also take on new beliefs (for example: 'The subject isn't really that difficult.').

Layer 5: (Professional) Identity

This layer is about the beliefs you have about yourself. In the example of the student who believes that mathematics is difficult, this belief can also be placed at this layer, for it might be that the student thinks that he or she is not able to learn the subject, and that this is a personal limitation. This is a fundamental belief, because it affects the student as a person; it affects the student's self-image. It should be clear that such a belief can have a big effect on someone.

The core question in this layer is: *Who are you?* To be more precise, the question is about who you think you are: How do you see yourself? When we focus on your professional identity the question is: How do you see yourself in your work, and what is your role in it? (If you are still a student, the question might be: How do you see yourself as a student?) For example, you could see yourself as a supporter of others, an inspirer, a hard worker, an executer of others' ideas, a critical thinker, a good co-worker, a successful professional, and so forth. All sorts of different ideas about yourself can play a role at the same time.

Again we can discern a mutual effect: beliefs about yourself (layer 5) affect your beliefs about concrete situations you encounter (layer 4) and vice-versa. For example, if you think you have good people skills (layer 5), you will probably be inclined to think that a problematic interpersonal situation or conflict that you encounter will be easy to solve (layer 4). If there are many situations which you believe you can bring to a good conclusion, you may develop a positive self-image in layer 5 ('I can manage a lot').

Layer 6: Mission

This layer applies to what drives and inspires you at your core. What is it you really want to go for? It is about enthusiasm, deep ideals, mission, your 'calling.' This layer has to do with the question of how you see your role as part of a larger whole, for example, the larger whole of the world or cosmos: What do you want to do to contribute to it? As such, this layer can also be called the layer of spirituality. For some people, this layer is strongly influenced by their religious beliefs. The core question in this layer of mission is: *What inspires you?* Again, the layers of identity (5) and mission (6) affect each other.

The Core

Finally, we get to the core, in the middle of the onion. We called this earlier the 'diamond inside.' This is the source of your core qualities. Ideally, these core qualities will be expressed on all levels, which takes us to the importance of aligning the layers.

Aligning the Layers

When all the layers are aligned with each other, you experience harmony within yourself and in your relationship with the outside world. There is often a feeling of positive energy, a kind of flow-experience. This can be seen as a flow from your core, which is the central circle in the onion model (Figure 7.2). Your core qualities are located in this core and they can be expressed through all the layers of the onion (from mission to behavior) and through this, the power of your core will be evident in the environment.

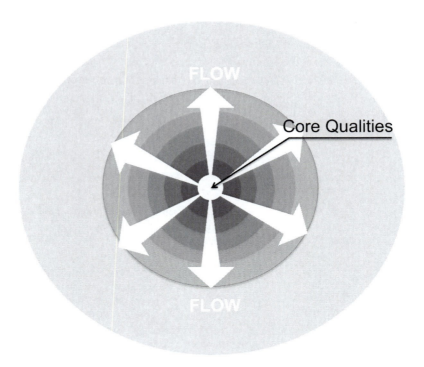

Figure 7.2   When all the layers are in harmony, you can experience flow from your core

A good example is Edith from the beginning of this chapter. Her flow has a positive effect on the people she meets. We will give another example in which you can see all the layers of the onion. A teacher wants to contribute to the well-being of the students and the school community (layer of mission). She sees herself as a future principal (layer of identity) and works hard to achieve this. On the layer of beliefs she believes that she has to put her full energy into all kinds of daily work situations in order to achieve her goal. This in turn influences the competencies she develops, which in turn decides how she can build a relationship with her students and colleagues (environment). Her professional development is in 'flow.' This flow starts at the core of this teacher, where core qualities such as commitment, care for people, perseverance, and self-discipline are present. These qualities then play into the different layers of her personality.

54 Introductory Activity: Recognizing a Friction between Layers

When you are not in flow, and you are struggling with something, the layers are not in harmony. There is a friction between the different layers. You can, for example, completely block yourself from following a personal dream (layer of mission) because of a limiting belief about the situation you are in (layer of beliefs) or a limiting belief about yourself (layer of identity).

Introductory Activity: Recognizing a Friction between Layers

Goal: Exploring frictions between different layers of the personality, as a characteristic of a problematic situation.

Materials: The onion model (Figure 7.1; see @, pdf #21).

1-1   Remember a negative (educational or work) experience and imagine you are in it again. Take the onion model (Figure 7.1). We will now go through the layers of the onion model.

2-1   **Write down:**
• What environment are you in? (Think about the space you are in, the people you are with, etc.). What influence does your environment have on your experience?
• What are you doing in this situation?
• Do you feel competent? If so, in what? If not, are you really not competent, or are your skills not being expressed in this situation?

• What are the main beliefs you have in this situation that are guiding you in that moment? (There is a good chance that these are negative beliefs.)

• How do you see yourself, your own (professional) role in this situation? (What do you think about yourself?)

• What is your ideal in this situation? What are you trying to achieve?

3-1 **Write down:**

• Is there a contradiction or tension between the six layers (for example: Is your ideal counter to your belief about the situation?)

• How does it feel to you to have this contrast?

• Is there something you would like to change? If so, what is it you would like to be different and what would you like to let go of to achieve this?

4-1 What core qualities can help you to make this happen?

The onion model shows that in working and learning there are always different layers that play a role, whether you are in flow or not. Sometimes you are completely unaware of these layers, even though they always have an effect. When there is friction between the different layers, it is more difficult for your core qualities to come out: only a small flow of energy is left (see Figure 6.1).

The three dimensions of thinking, feeling, and wanting also still play a role on each different layer. You can, for example, *think* about your skills, you can *feel* happy about your skills, or you could *want* to develop a certain skill further (and the same for the other layers).

The following activities help you to explore each of the layers of personality and how they are connected. We will also explore the layers further and help you to discover how they work out in your professional or personal life.

FURTHER EXPLORATION

55   Becoming Aware of Influences from Your Environment

Sometimes you experience a (work) environment as neutral, sometimes as very positive, and sometimes as clearly negative. You could question its effect on yourself and what it is you would like to do when you find yourself in a negative environment that you are unable to leave.

Becoming Aware of Influences from Your Environment		
Goal: Becoming aware of influences from your environment. **Materials:** None.	1-1	Choose a recent experience in which the space you were in (the building, room, classroom etc.) or the people in your space had **a negative influence** on you. Choose a situation in which you didn't leave, but in which you would like to change your perception of the environment. Imagine that you are in the situation again.
	2-1	**Write down:** • Where are you? How is this space? What does your physical environment look like? • How do you experience the air, the smells, the colors, and the light? • What is your experience of the objects in the room and your distance to them? • Are there people there, and if so, who are they, what do they look like, and where in the space are they? What is your experience of the people in this space? • Are there still other aspects of the environment that affect you somehow? How do you experience these aspects? • What are you most bothered by?
	3-2	Exchange answers and experiences. Help each other to further clarify answers.
	4-G	Discuss how an environment affects you (and potentially continue with Activity 56).

56   Changing Your Perception of Your Environment

How you experience something in the environment depends on your own observation. It is easier to change your own observations and experiences than to change your environment. Doing this is a choice you can make that can benefit you a lot. For example, the moment your belief about a situation changes, this also affects the other layers of the onion model. In other words, you are able to contribute to changing yourself and, as a result, your environment. The following activity will help you to become more aware of this.

Changing Your Perception of Your Environment
This activity is a continuation of Activity 55.

Goal: Discovering how you can change your negative experience of an environment you are in. **Materials:** None.	1-1	Go back in your mind to an environment you find negative (or take your insights from Activity 55 as a starting point for this activity). **Write down:** • How would you like to experience this environment differently? What would be ideal? • What would be different then in comparison with how you experience it now? • What would it be like for you to experience this environment differently? Would your perception of this environment be different? • What core qualities can you use to start experiencing this? (For example, compassion, initiative, vision, interest.)
	5-2	Exchange experiences. Help each other to connect to this change in perception.
	6-G	Discuss with the group, focusing on changing your own perception.
	7-1	**Write down:** • What are you able to change in your inner perception? And what are you not able to change? • What core qualities would help you to change your experience? • Do you have a concrete intention for your response to this environment?
	8-G	Discuss with the group, focusing on: What can help you to expand or change your experience? What can we learn from this? What can you do about your own experience of an environment?

57   Reflecting on Your Behavior in a Certain Situation

The following activity will help you observe your behavior. What are you doing? How are you doing it? What is your own experience of what you are doing, and how do others see this? Does what you are doing fit with what you would like to be doing?

Reflecting on Your Behavior in a Certain Situation

Goal: Becoming aware of your own concrete behavior and of how your perception influences your behavior.

Materials: None.

1-1	Choose a recent experience in which you did something or responded to something in a way that you didn't feel satisfied about afterwards.
	Write down:
	• What are you doing in this situation? How are you doing this? Why are you doing this?
	• How are you talking? How are you looking? How are you listening? Become aware of your exact behaviors. What are you really paying attention to in this situation?
	• How is your behavior affected by others' behavior in this situation?
	• How are you moving? What does your body language say?
	• What is the effect of your behavior on others in this situation?
2-2	Help each other to clarify your answers from 1-1.
3-G	Discuss with the group, focusing on becoming aware of behavior and the exchange with the environment. Interesting questions could be: What is your behavior determined by? How would you like to change?
4-1	**Write down:**
	• What is your behavior decided by? Why are you behaving like this?
	• Describe the effect of your behavior on others and the influence of your behavior on the situation as it occurred.
	• What would you like to change? What is the reason for this?
5-G	Discuss with the group, focusing on your personal experience.
6-1	**Write down:**
	• What would your ideal behavior be in this situation?
	• Spell out a concrete intention. Visualize yourself actually doing this.
7-G	Discuss with the group, focusing on changing your perception. Strengthen your image of changed behavior.

58   Reflecting on Your Competencies

Competencies and the development of competencies play an important role in our society and in education. Examples of competencies are: being able to write well, to speak well, to explain a concept, to structure a lesson, to hold a professional conversation, to gather information efficiently and to report it effectively, to give an overview, to organize and plan your work, to deal with conflicts, etc.

Competencies are usually developed through practice, and often through first developing sub-competencies. The following activity will help you to look at what you are capable of and what you are good at. We will also look at competencies (skills) you would like to develop and how you can do this in a way that gives you energy and satisfaction.

Reflecting on Your Competencies		
Goal: Mapping out your competencies. **Materials:** None.	1-1	List the competencies (skills, things you can do well) that you feel suit you well. **Write down:** • What are your competencies? • List at least four competencies. • How do you know that you are good at them?
	2-2	Exchange ideas. Help each other to clarify which competencies suit you.
	3-G	Discuss your reflections with the group. What does it mean to you when a competency really suits you and you feel confident with it?
	4-1	**Write down:** • How would you like to further develop the competencies you have? • What core qualities can help you to further develop your competencies (for example, enthusiasm, precision, persistence, compassion, perspective, etc.)? • What can you do to develop your competencies using those core qualities?
	5-2	Exchange your reflections.
	6-G	Discuss ideas with the group, focusing on developing competencies and core qualities that can help. Spell out your intentions.

59   Reflecting on Less Developed Competencies

It is usually not pleasant to experience that there is something you are not able to do. However, part of being a professional is to take a moment to look at this and take action. If you look at it from the perspective of development and growth, this will open new possibilities. What competencies would you like to develop further?

Reflecting on Less Developed Competencies		
Goal: Mapping the things you are less good at. **Materials:** None.	1-1	List the competencies that you or others think you are not good at. **Write down:** • What competencies are you not good at, according to yourself? • What are the competencies that others say you are not good at? • How does this idea of not being good at it affect you? • Are there competencies you would like to develop more? Which and why?
	2-2	Exchange ideas. Help each other to get clarity on what you are not good at according to yourself or others. What competencies would you like to develop further?
	3-G	Discuss your ideas with the group. What would you like to change?
	4-1	**Write down:** • How would you ideally like to develop your competencies? • What does this look like concretely? • What steps (and sub-competencies) could help you to achieve this? • What core qualities can you use for this? • Feel these core qualities inside yourself.
	5-2	Exchange ideas. Help each other to visualize this ideal, to experience the ideal situation, and to feel the supporting core qualities inside yourself.
	6-G	Discuss with the group, focusing on the core qualities that are important for the development of your competencies. Discuss intentions.
	7-1	**Write down:** What is your concrete intention for the coming weeks?

60   Recognizing Destructive Beliefs

This is a belief we have heard from a teacher: *Students are like flower bulbs, you have to put them in the ground before they will start to grow.* The teacher meant that he is convinced that he has to give them the proper 'nutritional' base. But the way he said it sounded a bit like: *Students are like flower bulbs, you have to push them down into the ground for them to grow!* This suggests the need to discipline the students to make them go in the desired direction. You can imagine the impact this may have on his class.

Your beliefs have a big influence on your work and life. This is especially the case for ingrained beliefs that repeatedly affect you without your being aware of it. This can be a very negative influence. Think for example about the effect of beliefs such as: "People are bad," "Life is hard," "My boss doesn't approve of me," "My colleagues are out to get me," "Work is not something to enjoy", etc. They harden you, blocking the free flow of your qualities and eventually limiting your growth. This is why we call them *destructive beliefs*.

The following activities will help you to become aware of your destructive beliefs and the impact they may have on you. They will also help you start to see your destructive beliefs as something that you are only limiting yourself with. As a result, this can help you to become less and less led by these beliefs. You could see this as no longer using an old computer program. This will make space for a new program to develop. In a sense, your internal system is then reprogrammed.

I am a bit odd	**I can't do anything**
Destructive beliefs 1	Destructive beliefs 2
I can't trust people	**I am not loved**
Destructive beliefs 3	Destructive beliefs 4

Example of 'Destructive beliefs' cards

Recognizing Destructive Beliefs

Goal: Becoming aware of destructive beliefs and their impact.

Materials: 'Destructive beliefs' cards (@, pdf #12), blank cards, the beliefs scale (pdf #22).

1-1	Take the 'Destructive beliefs' cards and put them in front of you from left to right (see the beliefs scale, Figure 7.3; @ pdf #22). On the left, place the beliefs that you think do not occur for you at all. On the right, place the beliefs that occur a lot for you. In between, place all the other cards. If necessary, you can write on blank cards any negative beliefs that are missing for you. **Write down:** • What beliefs occur a lot for you? How is this for you? • What beliefs are in the middle? How is that for you? • Which ones occur for you the least, or not at all? What is that like for you?
2-2	Exchange ideas. What beliefs do you recognize in your own life? How do these affect you? What are the influences of each of these beliefs?
3-G	Discuss with the group how destructive beliefs work. Pay attention to how some destructive beliefs can become dominating. Pay attention to their influence on your behavior.
4-1	Choose one of your destructive beliefs that you find undesirable. Imagine a situation in which this belief affects you negatively. **Write down:** • How does it feel for you that this belief has this effect? • Who or what is doing this really? • Do you have a choice in this? Do you have power over your beliefs or do they have power over you? • What core quality can you apply to be less carried away by this belief?
5-2	Exchange ideas. Clarify your ideal with respect to your destructive beliefs in this situation and look for the core qualities related to this ideal. Put emphasis on emotional experience: How does it feel to be determined by such an old belief and how does it feel when you let go of it?
6-G	Discuss in the group, focusing on everyone's discoveries and the intentions you have set.
7-1	Imagine yourself applying everything you have learned to your situation. What is your new belief? Ask yourself: What is the advantage of your new belief for you and for others? How does this feel? How do you want to proceed with this? Spell out an intention.

0% -- 10% -- 20% -- 30% -- 40% -- 50% -- 60% -- 70% -- 80% -- 90% -- 100%

Never --- Always

Figure 7.3   The beliefs scale

61   Recognizing Constructive Beliefs

Fortunately there are not just negative beliefs, but also positive ones. Think for example about beliefs such as: "The possibilities are always more than you can imagine," "My boss is happy to cooperate when I ask for help," or "A crisis is an opportunity." These are *constructive beliefs*. They give energy and are positive for you and your environment. The following activity will help you to look at your constructive beliefs.

Recognizing Constructive Beliefs		
Goal: Becoming aware of constructive beliefs and their impact. **Materials:** 'Constructive beliefs' cards (@, pdf #11), 'Body' picture cards (pdf #8).	1-1	Take the cards with constructive beliefs and put them in front of you from left to right (see the beliefs scale, Figure 7.3). On the left, place the beliefs that you think don't occur for you at all. On the right, place the beliefs that occur a lot for you. In between, place all the other cards. **Write down:** • What beliefs occur a lot for you? How is this for you? • What beliefs are in the middle? How is that for you? • Which ones occur for you the least, or not at all? What is that like for you?
	2-2	Exchange your reflections. What beliefs do you recognize in your own life? How do they affect you? Draw the energy of each of the beliefs on the 'Body' picture cards.
	3-G	Discuss with the group how constructive beliefs work. Focus on the conceptual framework that is connected to them and from which you act. How does it work?
	4-1	**Write down:** • Which of your beliefs are you most happy with? Why? • What is the impact of this belief on your work or life? • Which of your core qualities are activated by it? • Does this belief have an optimal impact? If not, what would you like to change about your belief so that it will create more positive effects? Pay attention to whether any destructive beliefs come up for you during this exercise. Are you tempted to follow them?

| 5-2 | Exchange. What have you become aware of during this exercise? What would you like to change? Verbalize your conclusions as clearly as possible. |
| 6-G | Discuss with the group, focusing on constructive beliefs and the 'celebration' of them. |

I am original	I am good
Constructive beliefs 9	Constructive beliefs 10
I love life	I am intelligent
Constructive beliefs 11	Constructive beliefs 12

Example of 'Constructive beliefs' cards

62   Changing Destructive Beliefs

It is possible to change destructive beliefs. However, first you have to be aware of them and then decide to stop acting on them.

Changing Destructive Beliefs		
This activity is a continuation of Activities 60 and 61.		
Goal: Changing destructive beliefs.	1-1	Choose a work situation in which you recognize one of your destructive beliefs (see Activity 60) that you would like to change.
Materials: None.		**Write down:** • What is the belief? • What effect does it have on you?

	• Do you have a choice regarding the effect this belief has on you, or is it in charge of you? • What core qualities could you use to be less dragged along by this belief?
2-2	Exchange ideas. Bring focus to the ideal and the core qualities in it. Pay special attention to the emotional experience: How does it feel to be led by old beliefs and how does it feel when you see that you have a choice whether to be led by them or not?
3-G	Discuss with the group: What have you become aware of? What will you do with this information?
4-1	**Write down:** • From now on, how will you deal with destructive beliefs? • What happens when you imagine that you are no longer being led by them? • Write down a new, constructive belief. • How do you feel now? • Where do you want to take this? Write down an intention.

63   Reflecting on Roles

At the layer of identity the important question is: What do you see as your own role? Examples of roles are: student, employee, son or daughter, subordinate, leader, supporter, team player, etc. You usually take on different roles in different situations. A role can empower you when it fits with your core qualities and your deepest ideal. But a role can also be limiting if it is counter to who you really are or your desires. It is even possible that you are given a role by your environment which you are not able to fulfill. This sometimes happens to pop stars or politicians, but it also occurs to 'normal' people. The central question is: How do you see yourself? And who do you really want to be?

In the following activity we will look at what roles you take on. To discover this, we will compare various roles, explore them, and look at which ones appear in your life. The leading question is: What is needed to turn the roles you take on into the ones that suit you well and fill you with energy? We will also look at situations in which you are limited by the roles you have been assigned or have chosen to take on.

Reflecting on Roles

Goal: Becoming aware of the meaning of different roles.

Materials: 'Roles' cards (@, pdf #9).

1-1   Take the 'Roles' cards and put them in front of you. Look at them one by one and see what the differences are. Put the cards in order from left to right, with those you find least pleasant on the left and those you find the most pleasant on the right.
Choose six cards (two from the left, two from the middle, and two from the right).
Write down (for each of these six roles):
• What is for you the most important characteristic of this role?
• Is this role important in your life (for example because you are attached to it, or because it occurs a lot)?

2-2   Discuss each of the six cards you have chosen and what you have written about them. What do you notice?

3-1   **Write down:**
• What is a role?
• For each of the roles you have chosen, could you indicate what its power is?
• Are there also roles that limit your ability to be yourself and prevent you from applying your strengths?

4-G   Exchange with the group and look at the strengths and limitations that are inherent to the roles.

5-1   **Write down:**
• What is a role you take on a lot at the moment and does it fit with who you are?
• What is your strength or core quality in this role?
• Is this strength or core quality optimally expressed— the way you really want it—or are there limitations due to the fact you have taken it on?
• Would you be stronger if you could change the role slightly or leave it completely?
• If so, write down what could increase your ability to display your power or core qualities.

6-2   Exchange in pairs. What roles did you describe? Discuss their power or quality, any limiting factors, and how you could express yourself better.

7-G	Exchange, paying attention to increasing your strength or quality. Verbalize your intentions.
8-1	**Write down:** • What is your concrete intention to express yourself more in your current role, or to tackle an existing limitation? • What concrete steps will you take to achieve this? • What does this look like when you are successful? Will others be able to see this in you? How?

Teacher Roles 1	**Child** Roles 2
Man / Woman Roles 3	**Friend** Roles 4

Example of 'Roles' cards

64   Reflecting on Identity

We will now take some time to look deeper at the layer of identity. Most people have different identities that are linked to different contexts. This means that characteristics of the person are applied differently depending on the environment he or she is in (La Guardia & Ryan, 2007). This activity will encourage you to look at your feeling of identity and what power it contains. Does it change in different contexts? An important question is what limits your power and what you can do about this.

Reflecting on Identity		
Goal: Becoming aware of how identity feels; experiencing the difference between the identity and your ideal. What core qualities promote your ideal? **Materials:** Blank cards, and possibly 'Environment, identity, and core qualities' cards (@, pdf #10).	1-1	Take three blank cards and write on each of them an environment in which you are active, for example your school/university, family, work, etc. **Write down** (for each of them): • How do you experience your own identity in this environment? 'Who' are you and 'how' are you in this environment? • What core qualities do you apply in this environment? • What positive impact does this environment have on the core qualities you apply?
	2-2	Exchange ideas. How do you experience your identity in different contexts? What are the qualities connected to the different contexts? What are potentially limiting factors?
	3-G	Exchange ideas. What are your identities? What are their characteristics? How can you turn around limitations?

65 Staying True to Yourself

We will continue to look deeper into the layer of identity. We will now have a look at the situations that are difficult or negative for you. What are you like in this situation and how do you see yourself while you are in it? The following activity will encourage you to look at this and make new choices.

Staying True to Yourself		
Goal: Experiencing identity in a negative situation. **Materials:** None.	1-1	Imagine an environment that has a negative effect on your self-image (i.e. the way you think about yourself). **Write down:** • What makes this environment have a negative effect on your self-image? • Why is that? • What happens with your self-image when you are in this environment?
	2-2	Exchange ideas. What in the environment do you experience as limiting? What would you like to be different? Do you have any ideas of what you could do to achieve this?

In (name an environment) ....

I experience my identity as ....;

important core qualities are: ....,

..........................., ...,

Environment, identity and core qualities

In (name an environment) ....

I experience my identity as ....;

important core qualities are: ....,

..........................., ...,

Environment, identity and core qualities

In (name an environment) ....

I experience my identity as ....;

important core qualities are: ....,

..........................., ...,

Environment, identity and core qualities

In (name an environment) ....

I experience my identity as ....;

important core qualities are: ....,

..........................., ...,

Environment, identity and core qualities

Example of 'Environment, identity, and core qualities' cards

	3-1	**Write down:** • How would you ideally like to be in this situation? • What would be your core qualities in that case?
	4-2	Form new pairs and exchange insights.
	5-1	**Write down:** • What is the tension in the situation? • What does this have to do with your self-image? • What core qualities can help you to realize your ideal?
	6-G	Exchange, share intentions, and get in touch with your relevant core qualities.
	7-1	Write down your intention(s).

66 Directing Your Work

The layer of mission has as its central questions: What inspires you? What do you live or work for? What is your purpose? In other words, what are you doing it all for? The following activity will help you to look at this in more detail. What makes your work or life purposeful and worthwhile? This question also allows for answers related to religion and moral perspectives.

Directing Your Work		
Goal: Becoming aware of what gives you a sense of purpose and increasing the power of this in your life. **Materials:** None.	**1-1**	Choose a recent inspiring experience, in which you felt self-satisfaction. **Write down:** • How do you feel about the situation now? • What core qualities are expressed in this experience?
	2-2	Exchange ideas. Give each other a brief overview (in a few sentences) of the experience and focus especially on what was so inspiring for you.
	3-G	Discuss with the group. Focus on the feeling of inspiration or purpose and observe the core qualities related to this. How often do you experience this feeling of inspiration or purpose?

4-1	**Write down:**
	• How important is it for you to be inspired in your work?
	• Are you currently living according to your purpose? If yes/no, how is that for you?
	• If there was something you would like to change, what would that be?
	• What core qualities help you with that?
5-2	Exchange in pairs.
6-G	Discuss with the group. Share your intentions.

SCIENTIFIC BACKGROUND

The Onion Model

The onion model has been developed by Korthagen (2004) as a variation to what is sometimes called Bateson's model. This model occurs regularly in literature on Neuro-Linguistic Programming (NLP, see Dilts, 1990). The authors of such literature refer to Gregory Bateson (1904–80), who in reality never actually described such a model, not even in the publications these authors refer to. So it seems that they are merely copying each other. Hence, the form we are using for the model in Figure 7.1 cannot actually be called 'Bateson's model.' This is why we have chosen the term 'onion model,' reflecting the different layers of an onion when you peel it. The onion model clearly represents the fact that there are different layers that play a role in human functioning. The outer layers (environment and behavior) are observable by others, while the inner layers really touch the core of the person. Korthagen (2004) proposes that the inner levels define the outward-facing levels, but that there is also a reverse effect (from outside to inside). The original title of the model was 'the model of the layers of personality.'

The 'layer of mission' is often referred to in the literature as the *spiritual level* (Dilts, 1990). This is seen as a *transpersonal* level (Boucouvalas, 1980), because it is about becoming aware of the meaning of your own existence as part of the bigger whole. Boucouvalas (1988) describes the essence of this level as "the experience of being part of meaningful wholes and in harmony with super-individual units such as family, social group, culture and cosmic order." This also means that on this level it can be about a deep religious experience, but also about a strong connection with humanity, the environment, ideals such as peace on earth, etc. In any case, it is about personal values that people experience as inextricably linked to their own existence.

The onion model forms the basis for a theory on learning called *Multi-Level Learning* (MLL) (Korthagen & Vasalos, 2005; Korthagen *et al.*, 2013; Poutiatine, 2009). This theory uses, as its starting point, the fact that in learning all the layers of the onion model play a role, but that the person is not always aware of these layers. *Core reflection* is fundamental in promoting this awareness and has been elaborated into an approach which is currently in use in many countries and at all levels of education (see Korthagen *et al.*, 2013, for more details).

Professional Identity

For a long time, the educational literature emphasized the importance of competencies. However, since the end of the previous century professional identity has increasingly received attention from educational researchers. McLean (1999) concludes that after decades in which 'the person' was largely absent from educational theories, suddenly a surge of interest could be seen in the question of how beginning teachers think about themselves and how they undergo the substantial personal transformations they move through as they become experienced teachers. A good example can be found in the work of Kelchtermans and Vandenberghe (1994), who studied the influence on the professional development of teachers of so-called critical life events, phases, and significant others. Due to the biographical perspective chosen by Kelchtermans, it became clear that the way teachers saw their role was to a large extent colored by the events and individuals in their lives. Interesting examples are presented by Mayes (2001), who shows how his student teachers' beliefs about the world and about themselves are shaped or inhibited by their upbringing.

A study carried out by Koster, Korthagen, and Schrijnemakers (1995) on the influence of positive and negative role models, brought to light clear examples of the extent to which student teachers were influenced by teachers in their own past. Those examples illustrate how past role models shape the professional self-image of people in education. This determines their behavior, for as Tusin (1999, p. 27) states, "behavior is a function of self-concept, which makes self-concept an essential aspect of teaching and learning to teach."

Underlying the literature on professional identity is the notion that personal and professional development are strongly intertwined. This is most clearly expressed by Hamachek (1999). Speaking about the work of teachers, he states: "Consciously, we teach what we know; unconsciously, we teach who we are" (p. 209). If we broaden this to all people in education, we might say that in their work, they all express not only their professional competencies, but most of all who they are.

Mission, Inspiration, and Ideals

In the onion model, ideals are considered a driving force in people's work, something which has also been stressed by Hansen (1995). While honoring teachers' academic mission, Simon (2001) shows how essential teachers' moral ideals and values are in education that impacts children's lives. Other discussions of the role of ideals in education can be found in Carr (2005) and Newman (2000). In his book, *A passion for teaching*, Day (2004) states: "Arguably it is our ideals that sustain us through difficult times and challenging environments; and it is our ideals that commit us to changing and improving our practice as the needs of students and the demands of society change" (p. 20). Palmer's (1998) book *The courage to teach* emphasizes ideals and inspiration and puts them in the foreground of our thinking about education. Palmer's book is a plea for taking our own personal mission and inspiration seriously. He shows that this is not only personally fulfilling, but also directly influences the quality of professional work. Palmer asks: "How can schools educate students if they fail to support the teacher's inner life? How can schools perform their mission without encouraging the guide to scout out the inner terrain?" (p. 6). Building on Palmer's work, Intrator and Kunzman (2006) speak about the importance of "starting with soul" and consider this as basic to staying healthy in your work in education.

The Changeability of the Personality

Some aspects of the personality give energy, for example a positive self-image and ideals, while other aspects can have a limiting impact. This has been discussed in detail in Chapter 6. This brings up the question of whether the personality is solid and unchangeable, or if in fact it can be changed. Following many psychological and therapeutic areas of work, the starting point of this book is that there are many things you can change about your personality. Our interpretation is that this usually works only if the desire to change comes 'from inside.' With this, we mean that you can change if you really want this for yourself and are prepared to apply yourself to achieving it.

8   Working with Presence and Mindfulness

You are teaching a class. The students are busy working on their assignments. You do your routines, but in your mind you are thinking about other things. So are you really there? Yes, you are physically there since you are walking around the classroom and observing the students. But where is your attention? Let's be honest; sometimes your thoughts just wander. Perhaps the situation you are in is not so interesting. Suddenly you're alarmed; you realize that you were 'away' for a minute. You are now trying hard to be more present in the here-and-now. But a moment later your attention wanders somewhere else. Your attention is always somewhere, but are you in the here-and-now? Are you really in touch with yourself, your task, and the people around you?

67   Introductory Activity: Experiencing Presence

Presence is a word that means being completely and consciously present in what is happening in the here-and-now. Presence is fairly rare in our modern day. The many stimulations from our environment often take our attention away. There are many ways in which your attention can drift and take you away from the here-and-now. For example, you can daydream, or actually be so strongly focused on only *one* thing that you are unaware of the rest.

Introductory Activity: Experiencing Presence		
Goal: Experiencing presence. **Materials:** None.	1-1	Take a deep breath in through your nose . . . Pause . . . Breath out deeply through your mouth . . . Pause . . . slowly repeat this five times. Become aware of your feet and let your breath flow through your body all the way to your feet. Take some time to do this. Be aware of your body. Look quietly around you and see the things in your environment. Listen, breathe consciously, and experience the space around you while also being aware of your body.
	2-1	**Write down:** • What is the difference between your experience before and after this activity? • Describe your image of what presence is.

68   Working with Attention

The previous activity has probably made you aware that you can focus your attention consciously on certain things, for example your breath or your body. By doing this, your attention is brought back to the here-and-now. Presence is the term for the 'state of being' in which you are completely and with your full attention present in the moment. It is also sometimes called 'being fully awake.'

It has been shown that presence has many positive effects, for example on the quality of work, and on people's wellbeing. In this context the term *mindfulness* is also often used. Mindfulness is focusing your attention on yourself and your environment, with full awareness of the here-and-now. So mindfulness and presence have a lot in common.

In the following activity we will look at the phenomenon of 'attention.' You will discover how attention works, how sometimes you can be completely present in the here-and-now, in touch with yourself and your environment, but sometimes not at all.

Working with Attention		
Goal: Becoming aware of the positive effect of attention. **Materials:** None.	1-1	**Write down:** To what extent do you recognize the following statements: 1. I often don't pay attention to the things I do daily. 2. Whenever I go somewhere I tend to not pay attention to what I experience on my journey. 3. I only feel tensions in my body when they are so strong that I can no longer avoid them. 4. When I eat, I often do so without being aware of the fact that I'm eating.
	2-2	Share your responses to these questions and look at what they mean to each of you.
	3-G	Discuss your reflections with the group. Spell out the essence of what has become clear by looking at the four statements.
	4-1	Remember a moment in which you had complete peace and attention. **Write down:** • What is the effect of this on yourself and others? • What core qualities played a role in this moment? • If this occurred regularly, what would the positive effect on you be? • What do you need in order to have more peace and attention?

5-2	Exchange thoughts, focusing on the question: What is the effect of attention?
6-G	Discuss your ideas with the group.
7-1	Write down: • Would you like to have more peace and attention? If so, at what times, in which situations? • What are the core qualities that help you to have more peace and attention? • How will you apply these core qualities in the near future?

69 Recognizing and Preventing Drifting

Having your attention focused on the here-and-now enables you to have better contact with other people and therefore be more effective in your work. In the following activity we will explore the relationship between attention and contact.

Recognizing and Preventing Drifting		
Goal: Becoming aware of shifting your attention. **Materials:** 'Being in touch versus drifting' cards ●, pdf #14).	1-1	In the next half an hour (e.g. in a conversation, discussion or course meeting) pay attention to where your attention is focused and on your contact with yourself and your environment. Use the cards to help you with this. When you become aware that your attention is drifting away from the here-and-now, write down the time and where your attention is shifting to. Try not to judge yourself. Only observe what is happening. After you have filled in your card, bring your attention back to the here-and-now. Feel your own body. Feel how you are sitting or standing and be as aware as possible of your environment, for example the people around you.
	2-1	(After the 30 minutes.) Take a look at your cards and put them in chronological order. Does something jump out at you?
	3-2	Exchange thoughts. Focus on: What happens the moment your attention drifts away? Why does this happen? Try to look at this 'non-judgmentally.' Is moving your attention elsewhere a way of making contact with something you find more interesting than what is going on in the here-and-now? Does it give you or take away energy? What is the difference with your experience in which you *are* consciously present in the here-and-now?

4-G   Discuss your reflections with the group, focusing on the theme of contact. When do you really have contact with yourself and your environment?

5-1   **Write down:**
- When do you 'lose' your attention?
- What happens with it?
- Why do you lose your attention?
- When that happens, what are you making contact with instead?
- What core quality/qualities do you need to apply (when your attention drifts to stay more focused on the here-and-now)?

6-2   Exchange thoughts and feelings.

7-G   Discuss your experiences with the group, focusing on core qualities that support the ability to be consciously present in the here-and-now.

Time:	Time:
My attention is on:	My attention is on:
I want:	I want:
I believe the reason for this is:	I believe the reason for this is:
Being in touch versus drifting	**Being in touch versus drifting**
Time:	Time:
My attention is on:	My attention is on:
I want:	I want:
I believe the reason for this is:	I believe the reason for this is:
Being in touch versus drifting	**Being in touch versus drifting**

Example of 'Being in touch versus drifting' cards

FURTHER EXPLORATION

Presence and mindfulness are about your connection with what is happening in the here-and-now, both within you and around you. Often, however, we don't really pay attention to what is happening right now. We are being led by our standard thought patterns and are acting out of routines.

70 Recognizing Automatisms

Things we regularly do, feel, think, and want, often become automatic patterns. This makes life easier, because if you have to consciously think about everything, you are not able to do everything you can now. But the flipside of this is that your automatic patterns and routines can start to dominate if you are not present or mindful. In the next activity we will explore how automatisms work.

Recognizing Automatisms		
Goal: Becoming aware of automatic reactions and their pros and cons.	1-1	**Write down:** • What are four situations in which you do things automatically, without thinking? • How are you able to do that?
Materials: None.	2-2	Exchange your reflections with each other.
	3-G	Discuss your ideas with the group, focusing on automatisms. How do you develop automatisms and how do they work? What power and benefits do automatisms have? What could be the negative effects?
	4-1	**Write down:** • What were two automatic reactions to people (reactions that you didn't think about) that, thinking back on them, you found clumsy or bad? • What led you to react in this way?
	5-2	Exchange findings.
	6-G	Discuss your reflections with the group. Focus on: What are automatisms in interactions, when are they clumsy, and why is that? When you look more closely at your chosen situation, can you see a more suitable response? Discuss how it would be to react from a state of presence instead of automatically.
	7-1	**Write down:** • What reactions would have been better in the situations you chose in step 4-1? • What can you do to prevent a similar reaction again when a similar situation comes up unexpectedly?

	8-4	Exchange. What is the advantage of responding less from automatisms and instead looking more at what is really going on? How can you make sure that you do this?
	9-G	Discuss your reflections with the group, focusing on: What are the ways for you to be aware of what is really going on? What can you do to make better use of these? What core qualities can help you with that? Spell out your intentions for becoming more conscious in the way you work with the advantages and disadvantages of automatisms.

71   Becoming Aware of the Pros and Cons of Downloading

Senge, Scharmer, Jaworksi, and Flowers (2004) refer to Brian Arthur, an economist in the field of high-tech products, who uses the term 'downloading' for the way we deal with situations through automatisms. We 'download' a certain 'solution' from our brains. This often happens unconsciously. Sometimes it is very efficient, especially in simple, practical situations, but often it is not, especially when situations are more complicated. Even so, we often hold on to this 'standard' way of dealing with our environment, even when we see things going wrong in front of our eyes.

In practical, everyday work people often try to solve issues through 'downloading.' However, this tends to lead to superficial and unsatisfactory results since reality is usually complex and the routine 'solution' that is downloaded will not always be the right approach.

Becoming Aware of the Pros and Cons of Downloading

Goal: Becoming aware of routine reactions. **Materials:** 'Downloading' cards (@, pdf #13), blank cards, sticky notes, and flipchart paper.	1-1	Take the 'Downloading' cards. For each card, think of an experience you've had that was similar. (If you haven't experienced something like it, skip the card. You can also write down other situations on blank cards.) **Write down:** • For each downloading card: What is your 'first impulse'? • Why do you have this impulse? • Do you follow it? If so, what do you do? • If you don't follow this first impulse, what is it that you do instead? Does the first impulse still have an effect (for example, if you do the opposite of the impulse)?

2-1	Now reflect on your answers to these questions. **Write down:** • What do you think about the reactions you wrote down to the last two questions in step 1-1? • To what extent did you have an automatic repetition of an earlier experience? Or was your reaction uniquely tailored to the specific situation in that moment?
3-2	Share insights. What similarities and differences did you observe?
4-G	Discuss your reflections with the group, focusing on the reactions and whether or not you are repeating patterns. What are the benefits and what are the negative effects of downloading?
5-1	What can you do to prevent yourself from ending up in download reactions that are not helpful? Choose a concrete situation in which, instead of downloading, you want to respond differently. **Write down:** • What do you want? How do you want to do that? • What is your concrete intention?
6-2	Discuss your ideas with the group.
7-4	Together, write down your conclusions on a large sheet of paper. Discuss which core qualities you can apply to prevent unfavorable download patterns. What can you do concretely in situations like this to respond in a better and more conscious way?
8-G	Discuss ideas with the group and spell out your intentions.

A student misses his appointment again ….	In a class a student asks a painful question ….
Downloading 1	Downloading 2
A difficult colleague wants something from you ….	You are in an incredible rush and you unexpectedly end up in a traffic jam ….
Downloading 3	Downloading 4

Example of 'Downloading' cards

72   Developing More Presence and Mindfulness

Presence increases your power while reducing stress. The following activity will help you to better understand the phenomenon of presence and mindfulness. Table 8.1 shows a few questions from the Mindful Attention Awareness Scale (MAAS) questionnaire (Brown & Ryan, 2003). The questions are about how consciously you do your daily activities. An important aspect of presence is, for example, that you experience your connection with your body. Please go to www.selfdeterminationtheory.org to answer all 15 items on the questionnaire and then complete the activity that follows Table 8.1.

Score these items on a scale from 1 to 6:

1	2	3	4	5	6
Almost always	Very frequently	Somewhat frequently	Somewhat infrequently	Very infrequently	Almost never

7.	It seems I am "running on automatic," without much awareness of what I'm doing.	1 2 3 4 5 6
8.	I rush through activities without being really attentive to them.	1 2 3 4 5 6
10.	I do jobs or tasks automatically, without being aware of what I'm doing.	1 2 3 4 5 6
12.	I drive to places on 'automatic pilot' and then wonder why I went there.	1 2 3 4 5 6
14.	I find myself doing things without paying attention.	1 2 3 4 5 6

To work out your score on the full questionnaire, simply calculate the average of the 15 items. Higher scores reflect higher levels of mindfulness.

Source: the Mindful Attention Awareness Scale (MAAS) (Brown & Ryan, 2003).

This questionnaire is reprinted in shortened form with permission from Dr. Richard M. Ryan. For more information, see www.selfdeterminationtheory.org.

Table 8.1   Mindfulness questionnaire (Brown & Ryan, 2003)

Developing More Presence and Mindfulness	
Goal: Becoming aware of presence and its relevance.	1-1 Fill out the mindfulness questionnaire at www.self determinationtheory.org and count your score. **Write down:** • What is your score? • What is going through you as you answer these questions?

Materials:	2-2	Compare answers and think of a definition of presence.
Mindfulness question-naire (www.self determinationtheory.org).	3-G	Discuss with the group and bring more accuracy to your thoughts.
	4-1	You can invoke presence by, for example, breathing in and out very consciously and calmly. Do this a few times. Move on when you feel that you are experiencing more presence. **Write down:** • Name some advantages of experiencing presence. • What core qualities are active in your presence? • What can you do to experience (more) presence?
	5-G	Discuss with the group your experiences, strategies, and if possible, start to apply them.

Stop. Breathe in . . . breathe out . . . observe

Figure 8.1 is a card with some words that can help you to experience more presence. You can find this card on @ in a printable version (pdf #23). You can print this card—ideally on gold-colored paper—and put it in places where you want to remind yourself of presence and mindfulness. Whenever you walk past, just take a minute to look at the card, do what it says, and allow yourself to be more present. That is all.

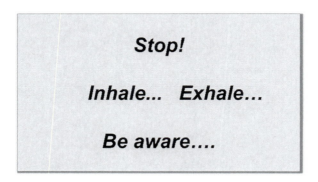

Figure 8.1   Card for increasing presence and mindfulness

73 Deepening the Connection

Senge *et al.* (2004) and Scharmer (2007) developed a strategy for professionals that is based on an analysis of successful processes in organizations. They call it *presencing*. This word is a combination of presence and sensing, and expresses a deep and complete perception of the here-and-now, beyond ordinary interpretations of the reality. The process of presencing is illustrated in Figure 8.2 with the image of the U-shape. Presencing is an alternative for the regularly used, but often less effective, process of downloading that we talked about earlier. When you are downloading, you retrieve on 'automatic pilot' a 'standard approach' from your brain that is often not so effective, for example in complex situations with other people. However, with presencing you are more in touch with the essence of the unique situation and with your own power and potential.

In the process of 'presencing,' the 'internal' (inner experiences of our potential) and 'external' (the observation of the environment) become connected. You experience everything more as *one* whole. Scharmer (2007) developed the process of presencing further. He supposes that presencing asks for an unprejudiced observation of the here-and-now from an 'open mind,' 'open heart,' and an 'open will.' So here we see again an emphasis on the importance of thinking, feeling, and wanting, the three 'channels' we thoroughly discussed in Chapter 3. Scharmer adds the key insight that it is important for us to keep these channels inside ourselves as open as possible. We are only really 'awake' once we can think about our current situation with an open mind, feel all there is to feel, and are completely open to what plays a role in our needs and desires, but also in the needs and desires of others. According to Scharmer, the most common factors that limit people to be open to this in the here-and-now are judgment, cynicism, and fear.

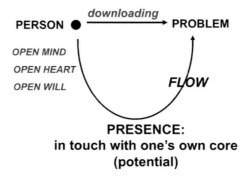

Figure 8.2   The process of presencing as opposite to downloading (Senge *et al.*, 2004; Scharmer, 2007)

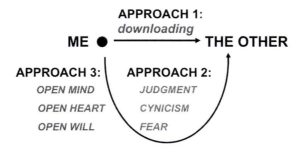

Figure 8.3   Three ways of interacting with someone else

Deepening the Connection

Goal: Becoming aware of your way of responding with and without presence.

Materials: None.

In Figure 8.3, you see three ways of interacting with someone else, for example, someone you experience as difficult. This could, for example, be a colleague, student, parent, or head teacher, etc.
Approach 1 is downloading (see Activity 71).
Approach 2 is giving in to judgments, cynicism, or fear.
Approach 3 is presencing—being present with an open mind, open heart, and open will.

1-1   Remember one or more situations in which you had to deal with difficult people. Observe if and how these three approaches occurred for you.
Write down:
• How do you respond when you are downloading (so more or less automatically)?
• How do you respond if you are acting from judgment, cynicism or fear?
• How do you respond when you are completely open (presencing)?

3-2   Exchange experiences.
Pay attention to the differences between these ways of responding.
What is the effect of these three ways on yourself and the other?

4-G   Exchange experiences with the group and focus on the different ways of responding. What is the effect of these different ways?

5-1	**Write down:** • What can you do to increase your interaction with others based on presencing? • What core qualities can help you with this? • How can you apply these with focus in the near future when you have to interact again with difficult people?
6-2	Exchange and pay attention to the core qualities that can help.
6-G	Share and spell out your intentions for applying core qualities.

74   Becoming Aware of the Timeless Observer

Your core is the elusive aspect of you that feels like your 'real me' and seems timeless. You experience the passing of time every day. You gain experiences and grow older. However, there seems to be a part of you that doesn't change, something that is just there and observes everything.

Becoming Aware of the Timeless Observer

Goal: Making contact with a part of you that is not affected by time. **Materials:** Paper and pencil for drawing.	1-1	Take a sheet of paper. Draw on it a timeline and write down '0' for your moment of birth, and the word 'NOW' for this moment. Place on this line three important experiences in your life. **Write down:** • Who are you in these experiences? • Who or what in you is the observer of who you are in these experiences?
	2-2	Exchange your answers. What is the part of you that feels timeless?
	3-G	Exchange, focusing on the power of the timeless observer. How important is that part of you? How often do you use it in your daily life?
	4-1	When you consider how important this part of you is and how much you use it, would you like this to be different?
	5-2	Exchange and pause to think about what you want and how you can realize this.

6-G	Exchange thoughts, feelings, and ideals.
7-1	If you feel that there is a lot of power locked up in this timeless observer, write down an intention to live more from a connection with this timeless essence inside yourself.

SCIENTIFIC BACKGROUND

Descriptions of Presence and Mindfulness

In the research literature, both the term *presence* and *mindfulness* are used (see, for example, Brown & Ryan, 2003; Korthagen, 2010a; Meijer, Korthagen, & Vasalos, 2009). A large part of this chapter is based on the work of Senge *et al.* (2004) and Scharmer (2007), who have made the concept of presence accessible for professionals. They also developed the U-theory that Figure 8.1 is based on. Riva *et al.* (2009) define presence as the state of being in which you are completely, and with your full attention, present in the moment. Greene (1973, p. 162) calls it being 'completely awake.' Within the context of education, Noddings (1984) and Rodgers and Raider-Roth (2006) have emphasized the importance of presence for the teacher.

Mindfulness is most commonly defined as "the state of being attentive to and aware of what is taking place in the present" (Brown & Ryan, 2003, p. 822). It refers to a state in which you have your attention completely on yourself and your environment, with full awareness of the here-and-now. Mindfulness is actually a concept that originates from Buddhism, but nowadays it is a skill that can be learned and is applied to the treatment of issues such as depression and phobias. It is also applied in mainstream medicine, for example, to treat pain (Kabat-Zinn, 1990).

Downloading

Presence and mindfulness are the direct opposites of taking action without awareness, or of routine and automatic actions. We call the latter 'downloading.' It is a regular phenomenon in daily practice because things we regularly do, feel, think, and want, become automatic patterns (Bargh, 1990; Bargh & Barndollar, 1996; Bargh & Chartrand, 1999).

Also Schön (1987) notes this phenomenon and supposes that practitioners are simply used to tackling situations from routine because of a constant pressure to act, but that these actions are not always effective.

Inside and Outside

In presence, there is awareness of your 'inner world' (your thinking, feeling, wanting, and body), the 'outer world,' and the connections between them. Senge *et al.* (2004) see building connections between the 'inside' and 'outside' as an essential direction for the development of humanity as a whole. They suppose that humanity has been focused too much on the outside, on manipulating nature, and 'using' the world. They argue that this leads to global catastrophes. They say that we have to learn again to experience that we, as humans, are *one* with everything. According to them, we wrongly see 'inside' and 'outside' as completely different. Einstein called this "an illusion of our mind."

Curiously, it was the most advanced physicists who came to the insight that in the cosmos everything is connected, even the observed and its observer (see, for example, Bohm, 1985). When we as humans no longer feel a connection with this larger whole, which for religiously oriented people could be called the unity of creation, our existence not only becomes empty and meaningless but our actions can even become dangerous. This is why Senge *et al.* (2004) propose that the most important element of a new vision of the world and humanity is *connectedness*, elaborating it as follows:

> [C]onnectedness as an organizing principle of the universe, connectedness between the 'outer world' of manifest phenomena and the 'inner world' of lived experience, and, ultimately, connectedness among people and between humans and the larger world.
>
> (Senge *et al.*, 2004, p. 188)

Senge and his colleagues conclude that "the only change that will make a difference is the transformation of the human heart" (p. 26). For more on this issue, see Korthagen *et al.* (2013, p. 195–201).

9 Turning Problems into Opportunities for Growth

Teacher Carolyn has the ideal to interact with her students with respect for their individuality. According to her, everyone has their unique qualities and people should try to see each other's qualities more so that they can contribute to a better world. She also thinks she should prepare her students to take part in a world like that.

Two of her students submitted an essay on volcanoes as part of their homework. The text is very slick and she wonders whether they really wrote it themselves. After a quick Internet search, she finds the exact text on a website. She feels cheated and gets very angry; she reacts furiously and tells them off. Afterwards, she regrets her reaction. She can see that she did not respond respectfully but doesn't really know how she could have dealt with the situation in a different way.

Carolyn decides to consult a colleague and wants to use the onion model in their discussion to help her reflect on the friction between the layer of mission (layer 6) and her actual behavior (layer 2) in this situation (layer 1). The colleague starts by pointing out Carolyn's core qualities; she mentions openness (since Carolyn instigated this conversation) and commitment to her students. She also asks about Carolyn's ideal in education. Carolyn tells her about her ideal of respect for each other's individuality. While talking about this she becomes aware of how she is affected by the belief of "I am being cheated" (layer 4). This belief invokes fury in her contact with the two students and is stopping her from behaving in the way she would like. Carolyn can see that she is being dragged along by this belief. She can also recognize a pattern; her belief of being treated unfairly comes up quite regularly and, when it does, it has a strong effect on her. From that perspective, Carolyn's colleague can now help her to use the elevator to find the feeling that Carolyn has about this: frustration and pain that she is letting herself get dragged along by a limiting belief and that this happens regularly. This takes the elevator to wanting; Carolyn says she no longer wants to deal in this way with situations in which she feels cheated. Her colleague asks Carolyn what she does want, what her ideal is. She says that she wants to interact with her students with respect for their individuality. This helps her to reconnect with her core qualities, namely commitment to her students and respect for people's individuality. This strengthens her ideal; she wants to act more from these core qualities, even in difficult situations. Her eyes are starting to radiate. She is suddenly very clear about what she wants to do. She wants to go back to the students and apologize for reacting so strongly. She wants to enter the conversation with respect and also ask her students strongly to pay more respect to her need for honesty.

This example brings together many themes from this book: the power of ideals and core qualities, the role of limiting beliefs, the onion model, and the principle of using the elevator between thinking, feeling, and wanting. Through all this is the theme of *presence*, which is fundamental to Carolyn's preparedness to look at the situation with an open mind, an open heart, and an open will, and to be 'mindful' and present to what happens during the coaching session. Based on this, Carolyn's colleague is in a good position to help Carolyn reflect on her issues in such a way that the connection with her core is restored, which leads to flow. We call this process *core reflection*.

It is especially in those difficult moments and in tricky situations in which you encounter a problem, that it is important to use the power of your core to tackle your internal obstacles that stop you from making full use of your psychological capital. Working from your core becomes a reality when you are able to use your problems as a stimulation to strengthen your connection with your core.

Sometimes you need the support of someone else. That person then assumes the role of coach. We will explore in this chapter what this coaching can look like and how you can use the principles in this book to support core reflection. Finally, we will look at the question of how you can apply core reflection to yourself.

75 Introductory Activity: Learning to Use a Problem as a Route to an Ideal

The first step is to learn to use a problem as a route to becoming aware of an ideal. Behind every problem is the desire for a more ideal situation. Discovering this ideal is a powerful tool for finding a new way of looking at this problem. We will now take a look at how this works.

Introductory Activity: Learning to Use a Problem as a Route to an Ideal

Goal: Learning to use a problem as an access point to an ideal.

Materials: Optional: 'Core qualities' cards (@, pdf #6) and 'Elevator' cards (pdf #2, #3, or #4), to be used by B.

Split into pairs. Person A reflects, and person B coaches.

A brings a (work) problem to the table, ideally one that is current and that A wants to progress in.

B has a coaching role and can help A by listening, empathizing, pointing out core qualities, asking questions, and occasionally summarizing.

1-2	B helps A to explore the problem. A describes the problem concretely, but without spending more than two minutes on it. In any case, avoid analyzing the problem at this stage. B listens, empathizes, and names the core qualities of person A that become apparent during the conversation. B then brings the elevator into action (see Activity 24): • What does A think about the problem (ideally in one sentence)? • What does A feel about the problem? • What does A actually want? What is A's ideal?
2-2	B helps A to explore the following elements: What is really the ideal of A? What would this situation look like then? What would A think if this ideal was realized? How would A then feel?
3-2	B helps A with the following questions: What core qualities does A experience inside when imagining his or her feelings in this ideal situation? What if A were to apply this or these core qualities in this problematic situation? Would A's experience of it change?
4-G	Discuss your experiences, focusing on: What helps to create a positive outcome of the discussion for the person being coached?
5-1	(Both A and B) **Write down:** • What has become apparent for you during the conversation? • What intention(s) will you take forward with you for future discussions about (work) problems?

76 Introductory Activity: Learning to Handle Obstacles

Sometimes the previous activity can help the person being coached (the coachee) to gain a new insight into the problem. In other words, they can get a new perspective of themselves in the problem situation. Sometimes this can even help to find a new approach to the situation. However, usually it is also necessary to face the obstacle(s) that plays a role in it, especially the *internal obstacle(s)* of the person: How does this person limit themselves in their ability to make optimal use of their inner potential? It is also important to know how you can manage these obstacles. This is what we will focus on in the next activity. You will go through the following steps together with your partner:

1. Briefly explore the problem.
2. Clarify the ideal.
3. Discover what limiting belief is playing a role.
4. Experience the ability to *choose* to be no longer affected by the limiting belief.

Introductory Activity: Learning to Handle Obstacles

Goal: Learning to manage internal obstacles in coaching.

Materials: Optional: 'Core qualities' cards (@, pdf #6) and 'Elevator' cards (pdf #2, #3, or #4), to be used by A.

Again, form pairs, A and B.
B again brings a (work) problem to the table, ideally one that is relevant right now and that B wants to progress on. Now A takes the role as coach.

1-2 A helps B to explore: **What is B's problem?**
B briefly describes the problem, but not in too much detail. Avoid spending time analyzing the problem. A listens and points out B's core qualities that can be felt during the conversation. Now the elevator is set in motion: What does B think about the problem, what does B feel about it, what does B want and what is B's ideal?

2-2 Look together for: **What is B's concrete ideal?**
What would the ideal situation look like? What would B think in that case? How would B feel in that case? Can B feel this *now*?
What core qualities of B show up then? Is B able to feel these *now*?

3-2 Look together for: **What is B's limiting belief?**
If B struggled with the question about what his or her ideal is, or is not able to imagine that the ideal can ever be reached, what is the limiting belief or limiting behavior? Try to summarize this in one concise sentence. Take the time to do this. Often the limiting belief has become so normal that it is unconscious. A can help to bring this to light and make it conscious again, because A can feel what is going on for B.

4-2	A supports B by using the elevator for the obstacle. What does B think exactly when they are stuck in this limiting pattern or limiting belief? How does it feel to be stuck in this (does B feel the tension that is created by this)? How does B want to relate to this obstacle? Does B feel they have a choice?
5-2	A supports B to: **Choose to no longer be led by an obstacle.** How would it be to not fight an obstacle, but also to not be dragged along by it anymore? Is it possible for B to, instead of staying stuck in the obstacle, feel that they have a choice to no longer be obstructed by this limiting belief? Can B choose to realign themselves with the ideal and the associated core quality/qualities?
6-2	What is happening now? Look at what happens sponta-neously and don't try to direct it too much.
7-G	Discuss your experiences, focusing on: What are the things that help to get a positive outcome from the situation for the person being coached?
8-1	(Both A and B) **Write down:** • What has become clear through this conversation? • What intention(s) would you like to take forward for future conversations about (work) problems?

FURTHER EXPLORATION

The introductory activities have clarified that for core reflection you follow a set of steps, a roadmap. You can see a picture of this roadmap in Figure 9.1.

In Figure 9.1 the fifth step is also step one again in the new round. This way the reflection continues, and there will be ongoing (personal) growth.

For core reflection a few things are essential:

1. The goal is not to deeply *analyze* problems, core qualities, or obstacles, but instead to keep the elevator moving (through thinking, feeling, and wanting).
2. Being conscious of the 'wanting' allows you to see your ideal.
3. This ideal has core qualities connected to it.
4. The ideal and its corresponding core qualities give flow, which might be blocked by (internal) obstacles.
5. Fighting or trying to change the internal obstacles doesn't help, because this just creates another problem. It is more helpful to look at the obsta-cle with unconditional love. It is possible to see through the obstacle completely as just being an obstacle and to decide to no longer be dragged along by it but instead to connect to your core qualities.

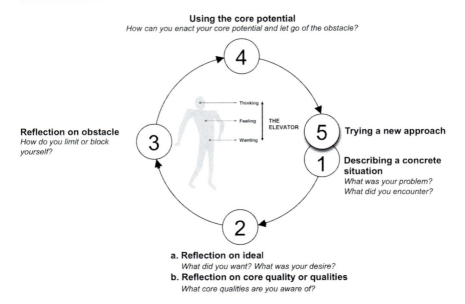

Figure 9.1   The core reflection model

Therefore, the aim of core reflection is not to *change* obstacles (such as limiting beliefs). This would only lead to more internal tension ("I shouldn't think anymore that I am being cheated"). The more you are trying to *not* think about something, the stronger this thought will become. (For example, try to not think about an orange elephant. . .)

In Carolyn's example from the beginning of this chapter, what seemed to help for her was to look at herself from the outside, as it were, from a state of presence. This then made her realize that she had a choice to be led by her limiting belief ("I am being cheated") or not. *That* is what core reflection is about.

This also means that it is not so important whether the belief is *true* or not. From one perspective it is true that Carolyn was being cheated. This is however not the essence of the situation, and the more you focus on the question of whether a belief is true or not, or the more you try to change a belief, the more difficult the process of core reflection becomes because the elevator gets stuck on the *thinking*. So don't get distracted with whether the belief is true or not. What *was* true in the example is that Carolyn had a problem partly because she let herself be limited by her belief. *That* is what deserved the attention, and it is important that Carolyn learns to feel what happens to her when she limits herself.

However, this doesn't change the fact that it can help when someone else (for example a coach) says how he or she sees the situation. For example, if someone is really stuck in the belief of 'nobody appreciates me,' it can certainly be valuable when someone, especially the coach, says that they truly appreciate him or her. The power of this is that it doesn't try to enter the fight of whether the belief is true or not, but that it just gives positive nourishment. This helps the person to see how the other person experiences the situation, and this can help to change the limiting belief. That would be a nice by-product of the process, but it is not what the process focuses on in essence. It is much more about experiencing autonomy: Is my obstacle or belief in charge of me, or am I in charge of my obstacle?

77   Leading a Session on Core Reflection

In the following activity you will learn to lead a full coaching session using core reflection. You will walk through the steps of the model of core reflection (Figure 9.1). In this activity we will explore the key points at each step.

Leading a Session on Core Reflection

Goal: Leading a full coaching session using core reflection.

Form teams of two, A and B.
A brings a (work) problem to the table, ideally one that is live, that A finds important, and that A wants to take to the next level. B has the role of the coach.

Materials: Core reflection placemats (the four sheets with the words problem situation, ideal, core qualities, and obstacle). (@, pdf #33).
The onion model (Figure 7.1; pdf #21).
Guidelines for coaching using core reflection (Table 9.1; pdf #29).

1-2
1. Put the four 'core reflection placemats' on the floor as shown in Figure 9.2 (@, pdf #25). Take at least 2 or 3 yards for this.
2. A stands on the sheet 'Problem situation' and briefly describes the problem.
3. B will now help A to walk through the steps of the core reflection model (Figure 9.1) by literally walking past the sheets. Don't forget to use the elevator at each step. The main idea is that from the left of Figure 9.2 (ideal, core qualities) flow is generated, but that this flow gets blocked moving to the right, and therefore you will experience problems. It can help to look at the layers of the onion to discover what the obstacle is.

2-2
After each step, or at the end of the whole session, A and B read the information from Table 9.1. Assess for each step what went well, but also whether the table gives any suggestions for what could be improved.

3-G	Exchange experiences, focusing on: What things help to bring about a positive outcome for the coachee?
4-1	**Write down:** • What has become clear to you from the coaching session? • What intention(s) do you take with you for future coaching sessions on (work) problems?
5-2	Change roles and run another coaching session. If you like, you can have a look at the text below ('Some common difficulties') and use it to your improve your session.
6-G	Discuss your experiences, focusing on: What works to bring about a positive result for the coachee? Also discuss how you can remain in flow as a coach.

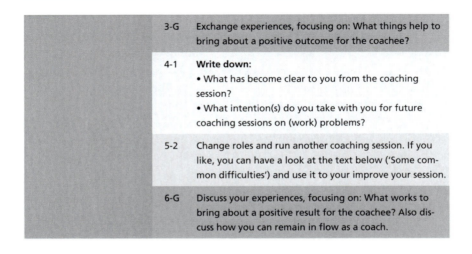

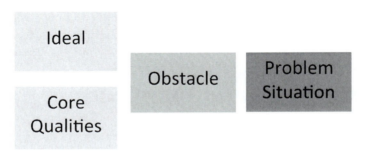

Figure 9.2   How to place the core reflection sheets

Phase	What is it about?	Competences	Tips
1. Describe a concrete situation or experience	The coachee has experienced something that bothers him/her. In this phase it is about clarifying the 'issue'. The coach *tunes in*. The goal of this is that a *connection* is created between them and that the coachee feels heard.	• Using the elevator • Empathic feedback (expressing the other's feeling) • Pointing out the core qualities • Giving I-messages (i.e. the coach describes his/her own feeling, how it touches him/her)	Don't let phase 1 take too long, because this usually doesn't bring flow to the problem. This phase can be finalized as soon as the coach and coachee are in contact with the problem: if the frustration is being felt, the question of wanting can be asked, which leads into phase 2a.

Table 9.1   Guidelines for coaching using core reflection

Phase	What is it about?	Competences	Tips
2a. Reflection on ideal	The coach asks how the coachee would like to have it, so what is the ideal. This has to be as concrete as possible: What does the desired situation look like exactly? What is the advantage of it (for you, for others)?	See phase 1	From the ideal you can often quickly deduct the key core quality (see phase 2b). Phase 2a will not be completed until *flow* can be observed. If not, there is not enough contact with the ideal, or its corresponding core qualities.
2b. Reflection on core quality/ qualities	This is about tapping into the source of the flow, i.e. your own core qualities. The coach can ask the coachee to name these, but the coach can also do this. However, it is important that the coachee really *experiences* these qualities.	• Recognizing and naming core qualities, and making sure that the coachee can *feel* them inside, and experience their effect. • Reinforcing the core quality, e.g.: "this is a very beautiful quality of yours!"	People don't get into flow only by *thinking*. Check the non-verbal behavior: is there *flow*? If not, there is not enough contact with the potential for flow and more attention needs to be paid to the ideal and the core qualities.
3. Reflection on obstacle	The core question is: What stops you from really going for your ideal? (and calling on the beautiful core qualities that are connected to it?) The coach distinguishes between *external* obstacles ("those people are being so difficult") and *internal* obstacles. Internal obstacles are often limiting thoughts ("I will never be able to do that") or limiting behavioral patterns (reverting to old and unhelpful behavior). It is essential to focus on the *internal* limitations. It is also important that the coachee gains insight into the negative effects of this (for him/herself and for others).	See phase 1 • Using the elevator (in a special way): - so you think . . . - how does it feel to think that? Or: - so you are reverting to that pattern of. . . . - how does that feel? - is that what you really want to think and therefore feel weak/ miserable? • Important are interventions that will allow the coachee to experience s/he has a choice: - so as soon as. . . . you think. . . .? - *who* thinks this at that moment? - who is responsible for this thought/ this behavior?	This phase will only be completed once (1) the coachee has become aware of limiting patterns, (2) can observe that s/he instigates these themselves, (3) *feels* how sad, frustrating or painful that is, and (4) can see that he/she has a *choice*. In short, the coachee has to start realizing that s/he is responsible for it and that s/he sets off the domino that creates the problem. It is important that the coachee looks at this from a 'distance', and chooses to *not be dragged into it*. Only thinking about the obstacle doesn't help! The person has to *feel* how s/he is blocking him/herself. Try to avoid that the coachee feels s/he has to 'get rid' of the thought or pattern, or that it has to change immediately. This will not be successful.

(*Continued*)

Phase	What is it about?	Competences	Tips
4. Using the core potential	Increasing the tension between the core potential and the obstacle: The coachee will start to feel the potential for flow and power, but also how s/he is blocking this flow/ potential. This tension has to become almost 'unbearable'.	• Using the elevator on ideal, core quality and obstacle: "So you feel how much you would like. . . . and that you have these beautiful qualities that can help to achieve your ideal? (check flow) And you are constantly blocking yourself by. . . .? How does it feel to do that?" (Or: "Isn't it frustrating to keep yourself imprisoned so much?") • I-messages, e.g.: "I wish for you to become aware of how much you are limiting yourself, and that you will stop being dragged along by it."	The trap is that everything can seem really clear now: the ideal, the qualities, the obstacle. This often leads to *thinking* about the situation and looking for a solution, both by the coach and coachee, and this stops the flow. This phase is all about *feeling* the contrast between feelings of flow (around ideal/ core qualities) and the frustrating feelings about maintaining the limiting pattern. When this contrast is strongly felt as an *inner tension*, this will naturally lead to a break-through: The coachee just knows what they want to do differently. If you end up looking for a solution, you know that the phases have not been success-ful yet.
5. Trying a new approach	This is about applying what you have learned to a problem situation: How could you apply those core qualities more, and no longer be dragged into the obstacle? (This is something different than 'getting rid of it'.) How would that feel? What would you get out of it? Do you really want this?	• Getting concrete: "so imagine that. . . . happens again, what will you do exactly?" (+ use the elevator) • Don't just check the new behavior, but also how the coachee now deals with this obstacle internally. • A mini role-play can help to strengthen the transfer. • Enforcing: "Beautiful! I can see you doing it!" (Only if this is authentic.)	It is important to check now: Do the coachee and coach have faith that it will be differ-ent from now on? As a coach, pay special atten-tion to the feelings (trust?) and non-verbal behavior of the coachee, and also make him/her aware of those. If everything goes well you should be able to see the person becoming stronger right now (and give feedback on that!). Again, if there is no feeling of flow, or if you are 'looking' for solutions, this phase has come too soon.

Table 9.1   Continued

Some Common Difficulties

When people are still learning to run core reflection coaching sessions, often one or more of the following problems occur:

1. Lingering on the problem for too long. The idea is to start using the elevator quite quickly: What does the coachee think about the situation, feel about it, and then, most importantly, what would they like? That question will then lead to the 'ideal' sheet.
2. The coach is so focused on asking the right questions and following the steps of the model that s/he forgets to use the elevator.
3. The coach is too focused on finding a solution. The main goal of core reflection is to see the problem as the reason to develop more awareness about ideals and core qualities and their potential for flow. This might lead to a solution, but focusing on the solution too soon is counterproductive as it promotes 'downloading' (see Chapter 8).
4. The coach starts looking for obstacles too quickly. Only when you can feel and see the flow that comes from ideals and core qualities (for example because the coachee is radiating this so strongly) is it useful to ask the coachee what stops him/her from being in this flow. The answer that follows is usually a clear description of the obstacle.

Problems 2, 3, and 4 usually occur when the session has already created some clarity. When the problem or ideal has become clearer, both the coach and coachee can become fixated on 'thinking,' especially about obstacles and potential solutions.

5. The coachee says, for example: "My insecurity is my obstacle." This is misleading because a feeling is never the obstacle but is actually a *result* of the obstacle. An obstacle is usually a limiting belief. This could be a belief about yourself (the identity level of the onion model). It can also be a limiting behavioral pattern (the level of behavior), but in that case there is usually also a corresponding limiting belief. So the *obstacle* may be the limiting belief "I am not good enough" and this creates the *feeling* of insecurity.
6. The coach is not in flow *themselves*, for example because they want to 'do it properly,' and don't give themselves the space to learn. Flow is contagious, and so is non-flow. This means that the coachee can only get in touch with his/her potential for flow if the coach is in flow. The key to this is for coaches to align themselves with their own core qualities, such as compassion, curiosity, intuition, sensitivity, empathy, etc.
7. Wanting to move away from using the sheets too quickly. People rightly think that it is not good to always have to "walk around the sheets" in

a coaching session. However, initially the sheets can help a lot in supporting the process, not only because you can see clearly where you are in the process, but also because the coachee can feel clear differences between the positions. Coachees often report that this was the most influential aspect of the process.

Activity 77 should be repeated regularly in real situations. Fully getting to grips with coaching using the core reflection method requires a lot of practice. In the end, it is difficult to learn the fine art of coaching from a book. Each coach has their own strengths and weaknesses in coaching using core reflection, and has their own 'blind spots.' It can therefore be useful in your learning process as a coach to get feedback from a professional who is competent at core reflection.

78 Applying Core Reflection to Yourself

You can also use core reflection to help yourself to use your problems for discovering your potential and for tackling your internal obstacles so that you can achieve more flow. In this activity you will explore this by applying core reflection to yourself. To support this, you could consider asking someone else to observe you while you are reflecting out loud and ask this person to give you feedback. In that case the feedback should not be about the problems or solutions but about *how you are reflecting*. What works well in how you reflect and where could you improve?

Applying Core Reflection to Yourself	
Goal: Learning to apply core reflection to yourself. **Materials:** The core reflection model (Figure 9.1, see @, pdf #24). Optional: The core reflection placemats (Figure 9.2, pdf #33).	1-1 Choose a (work) problem you find difficult and that you want to progress with. What problem comes up? 2-1 Now walk through the steps of the core reflection model (Figure 9.1), using the instructions in Table 9.1. You could consider putting the core reflection sheets on the floor and walking over them while you are doing your reflection. 3-1 **Write down:** • What was your problem? • What have you learned from this core reflection?

4-G	Discuss your experiences with the group. Exchange: What goes well and what is difficult in applying core reflection to yourself? Focus on: What can help someone to follow this process optimally? What are the limiting factors?
5-1	**Write down:** • What did you learn from this activity? • What is the strength of applying core reflection to yourself and what might be a trap? • What intentions do you take away from this?

SCIENTIFIC BACKGROUND

The core reflection approach has been developed by looking for an answer to the essence of psychological and spiritual growth. Hence, core reflection is based on several different approaches and theories about professional growth, such as Gestalt therapy, psycho-analytical approaches, psychosynthesis, rational-emotive therapy (RET), Neuro-Linguistic Programming (NLP), positive psychology, the Diamond Approach of Almaas, solution-focused therapy, and several western and eastern schools of thought. The challenge that the founders of this approach, Korthagen and Vasalos, took on was to summarize the essence of all those approaches in a maximum of five principles or a simple step-wise plan, following from the idea that most people cannot remember more than five things at once. Fred Korthagen also focused on deepening the core reflection methodology through scientific research, and many others contributed to this enterprise. This has resulted in several studies that mapped the processes and results that are inherent to core reflection, both on an individual and an organizational level. These studies were all brought together in the book *Teaching and learning from within* (Korthagen *et al.*, 2013), together with practical experiences and a new vision on education. We have summarized the main pieces of research below.

Individual Processes and Outcomes

Meijer, Korthagen, and Vasalos (2009, 2013) carefully mapped out what happened during seven coaching sessions based on core reflection. The person being coached in these sessions was a teacher who struggled with her professional performance. Based on analyses of seven audio-taped coaching sessions, the authors identified stages in the teacher's development and related them to the key principles of core reflection. The authors show that the teacher developed more awareness of her core qualities and ideals. The teacher started to reframe her previously limited and negative self-concept and her beliefs about the educational situations she encountered, which was quite an emotional process for her. She started to act more upon her core qualities and ideals, which led to an effective change in her classroom behavior.

Hoekstra and Korthagen (2011, 2013) also focused on the professional learning of one teacher. The authors describe Nicole, a veteran teacher, who struggled with implementing a new pedagogy requiring her to teach in a more student-oriented way. Detailed descriptions of the coaching interactions and in-depth analyses of Nicole's learning process illustrate that core reflection helped Nicole realize her ideals by drawing more strongly on her core qualities. As Nicole was also studied intensively before the period of coaching started, and data were collected about her classroom behavior and her beliefs before and after the coaching, the researchers found clear evidence of a profound shift that took place in Nicole, both in her beliefs and her behavior. In addition, the approach supported Nicole in accepting herself as a learner as part of her own professional identity.

A three-year study by Kim and Greene (2013) describes the impact of core reflection on their identities and practices as teacher educators at Southern Oregon University (SOU). The authors identify four themes defining the core identity issues in their study, namely understanding the contradictory nature of core qualities, confronting hypocrisies, holding ambiguity, and sustaining authenticity in everyday practice. Various categories of change in the authors' teaching identities and practice are outlined. Moreover, the study presents evidence of the beneficial influences of these teacher educators' own development on their student teachers. The authors conclude that core reflection serves as a useful approach for aligning professional and personal identities with a sense of purpose, passion, and teaching ideals.

Ossebaard, Korthagen, Oost, Stavenga-De Jong, and Vasalos (2013) studied the application of core reflection in a course for university students who suffer from procrastination, constantly delaying their work and therefore not making progress with their studies. These courses had been running for many years, but were originally more focused on developing skills such as goal setting and planning. The research study focused on the experiences of the students who followed the course based on core reflection. Research questions were: What did the course bring up for them? What did they learn from it? How did it affect their procrastination? Progress on the students' habits was measured using a quantitative instrument that was also used in the 'old' courses. The study showed that the course based on core reflection was more effective.

Processes and Outcomes on an Organizational Level

Attema-Noordewier, Korthagen, and Zwart (2011, 2013) describe a trajectory for professional development based on the principles of core reflection and carried out with complete teams of teachers in six primary schools. Quantitative and qualitative instruments were used for analyzing the outcomes of the approach for teachers and students and for the school culture as a whole. At the teacher level, the researchers found increased feelings of autonomy, increased self-efficacy regarding coaching of students and colleagues, increased coaching skills, new or renewed insights and ideas about learning, and increased awareness of core qualities in students, colleagues, and themselves. For most teachers, the learning process took place on all of the onion levels. At the student level, the teachers reported an increase in the students' working and communication skills and in the students' attitudes.

King and Lau-Smith (2013) explored the effects of courses in core reflection on the faculty of the School of Education at SOU. The teacher educators at SOU developed a multi-faceted approach to integrating core reflection across multiple dimensions of a secondary-level teacher preparation program, as part of other changes within the faculty. The study focused on the two-year process by which teacher educators integrated core reflection within their practices, the effects this had upon student teachers' sense of mission, identity, and behavior, and the tensions experienced by both. Finally, the authors analyzed the reciprocal impact that the transformations experienced by student teachers had upon the personal and professional development of the teacher educators themselves.

Conclusion

In the book on core reflection by Korthagen *et al.* (2013), more research studies on core reflection can be found. We feel that the studies brought together in their book form a strong empirical basis for the core reflection approach. In addition, the practical experiences described in their book clarify that the core reflection method can be applied both to students and teachers, in wide-ranging contexts, and in primary, secondary, and tertiary education. This is not really that surprising when we remember that—as we described above—the principles of core reflection have been deducted from widely accepted and thoroughly researched approaches on professional and personal growth. Core reflection combines the power of all these approaches into a relatively simple strategy.

10 Working with this Book

Some Practical Tips

In this chapter we will talk a bit more about how to use this book, deepening the section of Chapter 1 that focused on this issue. How can you get the most out of the book, both when you work with it individually and when you work with it as a group? We will also explore how you can make use of the activities as a teacher, coach, or trainer (in sum, as a facilitator) when you are working with people: for example, in a teaching or coaching project, a mentoring project, or in supporting someone's professional development, etc. We will give suggestions on how you can choose between the many activities in this book, how you can work with the different steps in each activity, how you can make use of the cards and other materials, and how you can support the interaction and learning during group discussions and in practice. We will also discuss how you can link activities to work and educational experiences in order to have the biggest possible impact.

How to choose the relevant activity

All of the activities in this book focus on developing the human potential, especially regarding core qualities and ideals, and recognizing potential limitations or obstacles. All the activities are listed by chapter in the table of contents. In Table 10.1, we give an overview with a different structure that is based on themes that people often come across. Table 10.1 lists all the activities in this book that might be relevant for that theme. This can help you as a facilitator to choose the right activity. Independent of the theme or problem, you can of course also start with a 'random' activity, because each activity has been designed to be independent and give insight on an important aspect of core reflection. The activities stimulate a process of developing more power through connecting with the core. To get used to the activities, it can be a good idea to start with one that is easy and specific. The orientation activities in each chapter are most suitable for this.

You can also choose an activity based on a recent experience. One way to do this is by walking through the following steps (that link in with the core reflection method we talked about in Chapter 9):

1. Is there a situation or problem that needs attention?
2. What is the ideal in this situation? Start by choosing an activity that helps to explore this ideal further.
3. Is there something that is limiting the realization of this ideal? Start by choosing an activity that helps to explore and tackle this obstacle.

#	Question	Description and suggestion of activities
1	How can I develop more focus and concentration?	Developing more focus (19, 20, 68), concentration and precision (9, 12).
2	How can I recognize qualities in others and myself?	Recognizing core qualities (2, 3, 4, 5, 6, 7, 8) and learning to give feedback (14).
3	How am I limiting myself in what I do?	How are you (unconsciously) limiting your own power (48, 60) and growth (29) and how can you change this (12, 54, 61, 62)?
4	What choices do I (not) make, and what are my dilemmas?	What choices do you make and why (25, 31, 34, 38, 39)? How do you deal with dilemmas (48, 49, 54)?
5	What are my ideals? What drives me and what are my values?	Discover your ideals (36, 37), how they show through into your life (38, 39), how you are (un)true to them (40), and what values you stick to (10).
6	How can I improve my inter-action with others?	What is your need for connectedness (32, 35), how do you recognize core qualities in others (4, 14, 15), what are influences from your environment (55), what roles do you fulfill (63) and what is your identity (64)? How can you work to make your communication more effective (24)?
7	I am not motivated, what can I do about that?	Wanting and having to (25), flow and increasing it (45, 46), calling on your ideals (38, 39, 40), calling on other sources of support (41, 42), tackling destructive beliefs (62).
8	What are my competences and what really suits me?	Exploring competences (58, 59) and core qualities (7, 8), linking core qualities to competences (6, 11, 12), exploring basic psychological needs (30, 33), and strengthening ideals (39), giving direction to your work (66).
9	How can I become more creative?	Different ways of looking at a problem (21), focus (19), clarity in focus (20), awareness and openness (68, 72).
10	How can I increase my com-munication skills?	Recognizing and naming core qualities (14), using the elevator in a discussion (24), recognizing core qualities of a group (15), unconscious habits (70), presencing (73).
11	How can I increase flow in my work and life?	Flow as an experience (43, 44, 45), core qualities and flow (46), applying core qualities that increase flow (11, 13).

Table 10.1 Examples of themes that the activities can help with

#	Question	Description and suggestion of activities
12	How can I get more energy?	Increasing the connection with the here and now (67, 68, 69), using sources of help (41), and strengthening ideals (37).
13	How can I increase my mental capacity?	How do you think (18, 19), what are limiting thoughts (60, 61, 62), and in what way can you increase the power of your thoughts (20, 21)?
14	What do I want and how can I learn to get better at choosing what I really want?	Wanting and having to (25), the need for autonomy (31, 34), using your willpower (26) and passion (27).
15	How can I handle difficult situations more effectively?	Person and environment (55, 56), behavior (57), skills (58, 59), flow (43, 46), core qualities (12), the need for competence (fulfillment and suppression) (30, 33), downloading (71), and presencing (73).
16	Who am I, who do I want to be?	Roles and identity (63, 64), core qualities (3, 13, 10), who am I in an inspiring or difficult situation (1, 65, 66), what do I live for (37, 39, 74)?
17	How can I listen to my feelings more and let go of limiting feelings?	Feeling (16, 22,23), the relationship between thinking, feeling and wanting (24), discovering and changing unconscious feelings and patterns (70, 71), using the elevator for ideals (39).
18	How can I become aware of what is bothering me and how can I affect that?	Limiting thoughts (48), fighting (50), fleeing (51), freezing (52), obstructing your ideal (40).
19	How can I contribute to a more ethical (work) environment?	Recognizing core qualities in others (4, 15), core values (10), contact, connectedness (35), presence and mindfulness (72), deepening the connection (73), the timeless observer (74).
20	How can I reduce stress?	Contact with the now (67, 68, 72), applying core qualities (12), looking at a problem through different glasses (21), the timeless observer (74).
21	How can I make sure to be less distracted?	Recognizing and preventing drifting (69), the awareness of thoughts (19), applying core qualities (8, 9).
22	I am experiencing a problem, but have no idea how I can find the solution.	Exploring the layers of personality (53, 54), different ways of looking at a problem (21), exploring a problem and the underlying ideals (75), letting go of obstacles (76, 77, 78).
23	How can I relax more in my work?	Exploring presence (67, 68, 72), changing your experience (56), the timeless observer (74).
24	I want to experience more inspiration in my work.	How does inspiration feel (1), autonomy (31) and how to increase it (34), exploring your ideals (37, 39), staying true to yourself (65) and giving direction to your work (66), the timeless observer (74), dealing with obstacles (75 to 78).
25	What can I do to improve the quality of my team?	Recognizing the core qualities of a group (15), bringing the core qualities in balance (13), recognizing core qualities in communication and naming them (14), fulfillment of basic needs in a team (29–35), improving the flow of a group (47), deepening connection (73).
26	How can I solve the disunity inside myself?	Discovering your ideals (37), using problems as an entry point to an ideal (75), increasing presence (72, 73), the timeless observer (74).

(Continued)

#	Question	Description and suggestion of activities
27	What do I really want with my work and life?	Core qualities that give meaning to your life (10), working and living from passion (27), exploring your own ideals (37), giving direction to your work (66).
28	How can I enjoy my work more?	Increasing flow (44), applying new core qualities (8), applying ideals in your work (38), staying true to yourself (65).
29	How can I live in the moment more?	Increasing flow (44), experiencing presence (67), working with attention (68), developing more presence and mindfulness (72), deepening connectedness (73).
30	How can I move forward with a problem that I've been struggling with for a long time?	Discovering your ideal in a problem (75), learning to deal with obstacles (76), applying core reflection (77, 78).

Table 10.1   Continued

How to Use the Activities, Both on Your Own and With Others

Reflection (and core reflection) can be done in many different ways, on your own, in pairs, in small groups, or in larger groups. If you are using this book on your own, you will only need to do the parts of the activities designed for individuals. You can recognize them by their lighter grey tint in the description of the activities, and their second digit is always the number 1. For the individual phase we usually ask you to reflect on a certain aspect based on something you have experienced. This reflection becomes clearer if you write down your insights. This is why we ask you to write things down in these exercises.

We have found that exchanging experiences and strengthening reflection through conversations is not only inspiring but also important in starting and continuing the learning process. Keeping this process fresh and new requires a wide variety of methods. This is why we encourage people to alternate between doing, individual reflection, exchanges in small groups, and discussion in larger groups.

An easy way to start the work in pairs is by comparing what happened in the previous phase and what was discovered and written down. But you can gain a lot more when the participants help each other to ask deeper questions and find out what can be uncovered. Some instructions you can use as guidance are:

- Listen well.
- Summarize what you hear so that you can check whether you have really understood what the other person has said.

- Improve how you use the elevator between thinking, feeling, and wanting (you can practice this skill in Activity 24).
- Keep asking questions, really engaging with what is going on for the other person.
- During the conversation, be in touch with your own core and with that of the other, for example by recognizing and naming core qualities (see Activity 14) and through presence (see Activity 73).
- Help people become aware of internal limitations (see Activities 48, 76, 77).

Occasionally the activities suggest working in teams of four. Usually these parts of the activities are used to collate the insights from the session into a certain concept or to develop a clear vision. Not only is it nice to see what others experience and discover, but it is also good to understand what mechanisms are at play in certain processes. Exchanging experiences in teams of four helps strongly with this. It is very important that everyone in the team participates equally. This is easier if the individual phase and the phase in pairs have been done first.

Using Cards and Forms

We have put together special cards and forms for many of the activities. Among these are cards with core qualities, constructive and destructive beliefs, all sorts of ideas, and also cards with photographs. The cards are very practical and concrete; they support imagination and connection to the theme. Cards are easy to handle, compare, arrange, rank, or select. They provide a way into thinking, feeling, and wanting. Always make sure that there is space for additional input by adding personal things on blank cards.

A pdf of the cards and forms can be found on the website for this book (@). Open the correct pdf and print as many copies as you need. If you are working on your own, you can cut out the cards and start working with them. If you are working with groups and are planning to use the cards more often it helps to laminate them. In that case it is easiest to laminate the full sheets before cutting out the cards along the lines. Keep the set of cards together with an elastic band. You now have a set of cards that you will be able to use again and again for years.

The Role of Mentor

If you are the facilitator (the coach, mentor, or teacher), you can use the activities in this book to support the growth of the people you work with. After all, each activity is a door to core qualities and strength. In addition, you can choose to let the participants use this book as a workbook. The advantage of that is that they will be able to read the underlying theory and get an overview of the important components.

To start with, it is important to look at what activities fit the current situation or the theme. It is always good to work on the needs and concerns of the people you work with. The stronger these needs are, the more they will be prepared to reflect and learn.

It is a good idea to ask the participants to do the individual step(s) at home as a preparation for the group meeting. The other steps can be completed during this meeting. The benefit of working in pairs, teams of four, and in the large group is that it deepens the learning process and opens up different perspectives. Your role as mentor will then consist mainly of improving the level of individual and group reflections. The group discussion can also be used very well for practicing new skills and to immediately implement an intention.

If you work mainly with individuals, for example as a coach, you would of course only use the steps of the activities for individuals.

Inquiring Together

The attitude that is demanded of the facilitator, and of the participants or students, could be described by something that Krishnamurti used to say regularly: "Let us inquire together!" (for example Krishnamurti, 1991, p. 215). He always emphasized that it is important to "inquire with an open mind, without drawing your own conclusion beforehand." This, however, requires facilitators to let go of the idea that they have all the answers and need to know everything. Instead, they should accept that no one can be sure what the truth is for someone else, especially not when it is about the journey inwards, to the essence of who we are. The teacher, trainer, or coach will need to be able to improvise and have an open mind, because when you are working in this way you can never fully predict what will come up for the participants and what theory will be relevant. It is important to go on a joint quest in which you let go of all preconceived ideas about how things are, and instead, look for what can be discovered and 'known from the inside' with a blank slate and fresh attitude.

In this quest it is important not to only use the thinking, because thinking doesn't necessarily bring us closer to working from our core. Thinking often refers back to the known, it wants to 'know.' The heart, however, often knows a lot more about what is really important to us, what touches us at our core, where our deepest desires and ideals are. This is why we believe that feeling and wanting are at least as important for the process of professional growth. So, it is essential that facilitators have the ability to not just ask questions that speak to the mind. This requires alertness, because in our culture it is the norm to ask questions such as "What do you think about that?" or "Why do you see it that way?". These questions slip out easily, but only speak to the thinking. Questions such as "What do you feel then?" or "How does this touch you?" or "What do you desire?" are much less common, especially in a professional context, even though they usually have a much greater impact.

FURTHER EXPLORATION

Facilitating the process

It can be very beneficial to work in pairs after the initial individual steps of the activities. Formulating your own insights and talking to others about this strengthens the learning process. An important aspect is that saying something out loud makes you more conscious of it.

To help the conversations be smooth and optimal, the facilitator will have to draw on some communication skills:

1. Recognizing and naming core qualities (see for example Activities 14 and 15).
2. Using the elevator between thinking, feeling, and wanting (see for example Activities 24 and 73).
3. Giving empathic feedback: empathizing with the feelings of the participants and articulating them.
4. Giving I-messages: being open about your own feelings helps to create a safe space.
5. Broadening the conversation by not focusing too long on one participant, but to say for example: "Who recognizes this?" or "Are there people who experience this differently?"

Creating Optimal Learning Conditions

When people are being asked to reflect on themselves and to share their reflections with others, it is important that there is a safe atmosphere in the group and a feeling of connection. This is created when the basic psychological need for relatedness is fulfilled (see Chapter 4). It is crucial to avoid judgment and cynicism and to not invoke unnecessary fear. It is also important that all participants, including the facilitator, try to have an open mind, open heart, and open will (see Chapter 8).

The basic psychological need for competence also plays a role. This means that, ideally, the participants know what will happen and what will be asked of them. It is also important that they regularly experience success.

The fulfillment of the basic need for autonomy requires being free to make one's own choices: being able to choose for yourself what you do and how you do it. This is why the activities have been set up to allow the participants to choose for themselves what they bring in and how. It has a reverse effect when people feel pressured.

In short, this means for the facilitator: nourishing connection, success experiences, and freedom of choice. By keeping an eye on the three basic psychological needs, working in a group can become fun and an atmosphere may emerge in which people can cooperate and grow.

Every person and every group has their own characteristics and qualities. The facilitator can put people together in pairs in different ways, for example:

- The people who sit next to each other make a pair.
- Numbers are handed out, and people with the same number form a pair.
- You work with colors or codes, and people with the same code form a pair.
- Specific people are put together based on experience, level of development, type of work, etc.

If there is an unequal number of participants, there will be one team of three. Teams of four are best created by combining pairs.

Using Guided Reflections

Guided reflections can be used to take a group through a relaxing imagination process. Facilitators take the participants on 'a journey'. The participants follow their own images and associations during this guided reflection and come in contact with aspects that are important to them. Guided reflections help to strengthen the connection with the inner experience of situations and to use the channels of thinking, feeling, and wanting. This calls on 'the whole person,' especially if people also have the freedom to not just express their reflection through analytical language, but also through drawing or poetry.

We will give an example. If as a facilitator you want to focus on the theme 'inspiration,' this is what a guided reflection might look like:

- I will now lead a reflection that everyone can do for themselves. This reflection will especially draw on your right brain, the side that doesn't use analytical thought but operates through imagery.
- There is not *one* way of doing this. It is about your personal experience. If I say something that doesn't fit your reflection at that moment, you can just let it go.
- Sit down nice and relaxed. (*pause*) Breathe a few times, deep in through your nose and slowly out through your mouth. If you like, you can close your eyes. If you don't want to, you can just keep them open.
- Feel how your feet touch the ground and how you sit on the chair. (*pause*) Slowly focus your attention on different parts of your body, working your way all the way down. Take your time to do this.
- Now go back in memory to a recent work experience in which you had a feeling of "wow", a notion of "Yes, this is how I want to work!" (*pause*) If you regularly experience this, just choose one that is very clear for you right now.
- Visualize this situation in front of you, as if you are in it again. (*pause*) Allow the image to become clearer. (*pause*) What do you see? (*pause*)
- What do you hear? Listen to what is being said, and especially how this is being said. (*pause*)
- How do you feel? (*pause*) How are you touched by what is happening? (*pause*) What gives you the experience of "wow"? What is it that inspires you in this situation and that you often long for in your work? (*pause*)
- Take a few moments to write something down about this, or—if you prefer—make a drawing of what inspires you in your work.

Very often a guided reflection starts by connecting with the breath, becoming aware of the body, and focusing on the here-and-now. A state of presence can be invoked by breathing in slowly through the nose and out through the mouth a few times. Thoughts calm down, which allows the channels of feeling and wanting to open up more easily. If a group gets used to this, the awareness of the body can be further increased by, for example, asking people to feel where the body feels relaxed, and where there is tension. It is valuable to learn to become more aware of the body, because our body often tells us a lot about what is happening with us. So there are multiple benefits to starting a guided reflection with an awareness of the body.

If you are the one leading a guided reflection, it is a good idea to do this at a slow speed. Give the participants enough time to connect with what is raised. It also helps to participate in the reflection yourself, while you are leading it, because you may notice that sometimes you need more time to connect with the topic than you expected.

Improving Transfer

Many activities end with the question of writing down an intention. This is important for increasing the transfer to the everyday work (see Chapter 1), but often it is not enough. People tend to forget their intention when they are back in their day-to-day activities. They easily return to their old patterns. There-fore, changing a habit requires more focus. The way to stimulate a behavioral change is by 'anchoring' the desired change, for example, using one of the fol-lowing methods: (1) leading a reflection in several stages; (2) writing down the intentions on a card; (3) the 'Do it *now*' exercise; (4) role plays and simulations; and (5) creative tools. We will discuss each of these methods in turn.

1.   Leading a Reflection in Several Stages
A reflection that is focused on transfer could go as follows: "See yourself in a situation in which you are successfully following your intention. Allow the image to become clearer (*pause*) and see in front of you in much detail what you are doing exactly and the positive things that are happening. You might get a feeling of unfamiliarity if you are not used to behaving that way. Accept this feeling, because it is part of you extending your comfort zone. But also be aware of how you get a positive feeling when you act out your intention. Con-sciously connect with that feeling. (*Pause*) What core quality do you feel right now in acting out your intention? Allow a symbol of this core quality to come up (for example a flower, a river, an open space, a heart, a bird, a stone . . .). Just observe the image that is coming up, and don't analyze it. (*Pause*) Draw this symbol. (*The participants could also, for example, put down their drawings in a circle and share their experiences.*) Take the drawing home with you and hang it up someplace where you will regularly be reminded of it."

2.   Writing Down an Intention on a Card
Everyone writes down their intention on a card and the participants make sure they see this daily, for example by putting it in their diary or by putting it somewhere in their workplace where they can see it clearly. By reminding yourself of your intention on a daily basis you increase the chance that you will really implement it.

3.   Do It Now
More intrusive (and therefore stimulating transfer) is to show the intended behavior in the here-and-now. We call this exercise 'Do it *now*.' The person guiding the group asks the participants to translate their intention into

concrete behavior and to write this behavior on a card with a pen in *one* sentence or a few words. They put this card in front of them so that it is also visible to the whole group. They also tell the group what intended behavior is written on the card. The facilitator will then announce a topic for discussion or another relevant activity in which the challenge for everybody is to do what is written on the card. In other words, the new behavior is no longer postponed to another day in the workplace, but the participants practice with this new behavior in the here-and-now. This often leads to a very stimulating and exciting happening in which everyone has to cross a barrier that they might never take otherwise. This method also allows the facilitator to briefly coach individual members of the group who might not easily cross this barrier, or to ask the participants to take a time-out and coach each other in pairs.

Let us consider an example. Mike wants to ask his colleagues more questions about their feelings. He puts a card in front of him saying "More feeling questions." While the group discusses the chosen topic, the facilitator notices that Mike does not ask any questions about feelings. The facilitator asks for a time-out and starts to coach Mike. Using the core reflection approach, he helps Mike to re-connect with the ideal on his card and helps him identify a core quality that could support him. Mike discovers that he wants to use more courage. The facilitator asks him what he would do differently during the group discussion if he would act upon his courage. Mike's body language shows that he becomes enthusiastic and more ready to act. The facilitator asks Mike to formulate a concrete question he actually wants to put to another group member. The time-out ends in a natural way when Mike turns to another participant (Sally) and asks for her feelings about the group conversation. The facilitator says "Yes!," while Sally starts to answer the question. Next, the group discussion continues. During the next five minutes, Mike asks more feeling questions.

4. Role-plays and Simulations

Another powerful way to practice behavior in the here-and-now in order to improve transfer is by using a role-play or simulation. One or more people play someone from the practical situation of the participant, and this participant practices the intended behavior. It can help to slowly increase the difficulty by starting with an easy situation before playing out a more complex case.

5. Creative Tools

Intentions can be incorporated into all sorts of creative tools. This has an important value, because our consciousness reacts strongly to influences that are being processed through experiences (see Chapter 3). This experiential system works through feelings, images, movement, sound, music, etc. The facilitator could for example turn on a rhythmic piece of music and ask everyone to repeat the intention to the beat. Sentences can be shortened or adjusted to make this easier. The challenge is to make it swing.

Intentions can also be expressed through a song or sound game. Group members might read out pieces of text after each other, or through each other, while moving or dancing. This can lead to a small party in which the intentions are 'celebrated.'

Finally, intentions can also be incorporated into drawings, paintings, posters, or photographs in combination with text or without words. The result can then be hung in a clearly visible place.

Peer-coaching

An important way to promote an ongoing learning process is by organizing peer-coaching. The participants come together every now and then in pairs or teams of three to coach each other and apply what they have learned. The trick is to make these get-togethers fun but also to bring structure into the coaching so that the learning is really strengthened. The participants could, for example, use the method of core reflection (see Chapter 9). The learning process can be further improved if the participants write a little report about the peer-coaching. Sometimes it can be good for the continuation of the learning process of the whole group if these reports are sent around, but only if enough safety has been created in the group.

Further Development as a Teacher or Coach

Teachers or coaches who want to get better at supporting people's growth process can find many exercises and insights in this book that can help them become better facilitators. If this brings up the desire to learn more about how to become a better facilitator, it will be good to know that the pedagogical approach underlying this book is called the *realistic pedagogy*. This pedagogical approach has been described in more detail in Korthagen *et al.* (2001). At the core of the realistic approach is that the learner's own experiences form the basis for reflection and the introduction of theory. Workshops are being given on the realistic approach, including workshops on how to work with this book. Of course, in such workshops the realistic approach is not only content, but it also shapes the way the workshop is given. This gives participants the opportunity to *experience* the realistic approach, which helps to create a sound basis for learning how to use the approach.

A crucial aspect of the realistic approach is the focus on core reflection. Hence, it is helpful if a facilitator is competent in promoting such reflection. There are also specific workshops on coaching based on core reflection. Increasingly, they are given all over the world. For more information, see www.korthagen.nl.

SCIENTIFIC BACKGROUND

The educational and pedagogical insights described in this chapter are based on research on effective learning and facilitating learning processes. For example, nowadays the literature emphasizes the need for creating *communities of learners*, a concept developed by Wenger (1988). Many studies have shown the positive outcomes of such communities. This book makes use of several principles of this approach, such as:

1. Take your participants seriously as partners in the process of building knowledge.
2. Promote collaboration and give responsibility to the participants for processes and outcomes.
3. Promote reflection and inquiry.
4. Make sure that supporting materials and further insights are available.

The way we have designed this book is based on the *pedagogy of realistic education*. This approach was developed in the context of teacher education and its effects have been thoroughly researched and described. According to Korthagen *et al.* (2001, p. 257) the five assumptions underlying this pedagogy are:

1. Start with concrete, practical problems and concerns experienced by the participants in real situations.
2. Encourage the participants to systematically reflect on the thinking, feeling, wanting, and acting of themselves and the people they work with, on the role of the context, and on the relationships between those aspects.
3. Stimulate the interaction between the teacher (trainer) and the participants and promote interactions among the participants.

4.   Take the theory on levels of learning into account (Korthagen &
     Lagerwerf, 2001). This means building the learning process
     according to three consecutive levels:

     •   Images and experiences from practice (so called *Gestalts*);
     •   Concepts and principles that give structure to these images
         and experiences (so-called *cognitive schemata*);
     •   (scientific) theory.

     You may notice that the chapters of this book have also been writ-
     ten according to this structure.

5.   Promote the integration of practice and theory and the integra-
     tion of various disciplines.

Multiple studies into the application of the realistic approach in teacher
education have shown that it leads to positive outcomes (Korthagen,
2010c). In particular, it improves the integration of theory and practice
and therefore the transfer of knowledge to practice (Brouwer & Korthagen,
2005). For more information about the empirical background of the realistic approach we refer to Korthagen *et al.* (2001), which is a book that
has been translated into many other languages (see www.korthagen.nl).
For a brief overview of the basic ideas of realistic teacher education,
including many ideas about how to promote reflection, see Korthagen
and Kessels (1999) and Korthagen (2010b, 2010c). On the topic of promoting core reflection we refer to Korthagen *et al.* (2013).

References

Almaas, A. H. (1986). *Essence: The diamond approach to inner realization*. York Beach, ME: Red Wheel Weiser.

Almaas, A. H. (1998). *The pearl beyond price*. Berkeley, CA: Diamond Books.

Altarriba, J., Basnight, D. M., & Canary, T. M. (2003). Emotion representation and perception across cultures. *Online Readings in Psychology and Culture, 4*(1), http://dx.doi.org/10.9707/2307-0919.1033.

Armfield, J. M. (2006). Cognitive vulnerability: A model of the etiology of fear. *Clinical Psychology Review, 26*, 746–768.

Aspinwall, L. G. & Staudinger, U. M. (Eds.). (2003). *A psychology of human strengths: Fundamental questions and future directions for a positive psychology*. Washington, DC: American Psychological Association.

Attema-Noordewier, S., Korthagen, F. & Zwart, R. (2011). Promoting quality from within: A new perspective on professional development in schools. In M. Kooy & K. van Veen (Eds.), *Teacher learning that matters: International perspectives* (pp. 115–142). New York: Routledge.

Attema-Noordewier, S., Korthagen, F.A.J., & Zwart, R. C. (2013). Core reflection in primary schools: A new approach to educational innovation. In F. A. J. Korthagen, Y. M. Kim, & W. L. Greene, *Teaching and learning from within: A core reflection approach to quality and inspiration in education* (pp. 111–130). New York/London: Routledge.

Bakker, A. B. (2005). Flow among music teachers and their students: The crossover of peak experiences. *Journal of Vocational Behavior, 26*–44.

Bargh, J. A. (1990). Auto-motives: Preconscious determinants of social interaction. In E. T. Higgins & R. M. Sorrentino (Eds.), *Handbook of motivation and cognition: Foundations of social behavior* (Vol. 2, pp. 93–130). New York: The Guildford Press.

Bargh, J. A. & Barndollar, K. (1996). Automaticy in action: The unconscious as repository of chronic goals and motives. In P. M. Gollwitzer & J. A. Bargh (Eds.), *The psychology of action: Linking cognition and motivation to behavior* (pp. 457–481). New York: The Guilford Press.

Bargh, J. A. & Chartrand, T. L. (1999). The unbearable automaticity of being. *American Psychologist, 54*(7), 462–479.

Bargh, J. A. & Ferguson, M. J. (2000). Beyond behaviorism: On the automaticity of higher mental processes. *Psychological Bulletin, 126*(6), 925–945.

Baumeister, R. & Leary, M. R. (1995). The need to belong: Desire for interpersonal attachments as a fundamental human motivation. *Psychological Bulletin, 117*, 497–529.

Bohm, D. (1985). *Wholeness and the implicate order*. London: Routledge.

Boucouvalas, M. (1980). Transpersonal psychology: A working outline of the field. *Journal of Transpersonal Psychology, 12*(1), 37–46.

Boucouvalas, M. (1988). An analysis and critique of the concept "self" in self-directed learning: Toward a more robust construct for research and practice. In M. Zukas (Ed.), *Proceedings of the Trans-Atlantic Dialogue Conference* (pp. 56–61). Leeds, England: University of Leeds.

Boyer, W. (2006). Accentuate the positive. *Journal of Research in Childhood Education, 21*(1), 53–63.

Bracha, H. S. (2004). Freeze, flight, fight, fright, faint: Adaptationist perspectives on the acute stress response spectrum. *CNS Spectrums, 9,* 679–685.

Brand, S., Reimer, T., & Opwis, K. (2007). How do we learn in a negative mood? Effects of a negative mood on transfer and learning. *Learning and Instruction, 17,* 1–16.

Brouwer, N. & Korthagen, F. (2005). Can teacher education make a difference? *American Educational Research Journal, 42*(1), 153–224.

Brown, J. S., Collins, A., & Duguid, P. (1989). Situated cognition and the culture of learning. *Educational Researcher,* 32–42.

Brown, K. W. & Ryan, R. (2003). The benefits of being present: Mindfulness and its role in psychological well-being. *Journal of Personality and Social Psychology, 84*(4), 822–848.

Brown, N. J., Sokal, A. D., & Friedman, H. L. (2013). The complex dynamics of wishful thinking: The critical positivity ratio. *American Psychologist, 68*(9), 801–813.

Carr, D. (2005). Professional and personal values and virtues in education and teaching. *Oxford Review of Education, 32*(2), 171–183.

Chen, K., Yen, D. C., Hung, S., & Huang, A. (2008). An exploratory study of the selection of communication media: The relationship between flow and communication outcomes. *Decision Support Systems, 45*(4), 822–832.

Cipriani, G. P. & Makris, M. (2006). A model with self-fulfilling prophecies of longevity. *Economics Letters, 91,* 122–126.

Confer, J. C., Easton, J. A., Fleischman, D. S., Goetz, C. D., Lewis, D.M.G., Perilloux, C., & Buss. D. M. (2010). Evolutionary psychology, controversies, questions, prospects, and limitations. *American Psychologist, 65,* 110–126.

Corr, P. J. (2010). The psychoticism–psychopathy continuum: A neuropsychological model of core deficits. *Personality and Individual Differences, 48,* 695–703.

Csikszentmihalyi, M. (1990). *Flow: The psychology of optimal experience.* New York: Harper.

Csikszentmihalyi, M. (1992). Imagining the self: An evolutionary excursion. *Poetics, 21,* 153–167.

Csikszentmihalyi, M. (1993). *The evolving self, a psychology for the third millennium.* New York: Harper.

Csikszentmihalyi, M. (1997). *Finding flow: The psychology of engagement with everyday life.* Basic Books.

Dahlsgaard, K., Peterson, C., & Seligman, M. (2005). Shared virtue: The convergence of valued human strengths across culture and history. *Review of General Psychology, 9*(13), 203–213.

Damasio, A. (1999). *The feeling of what happens: Body and emotion in the making of consciousness.* London: Heinemann.

Day, C. (2004). *A passion for teaching.* London: Taylor & Francis.

De Bono, E. (1985). *Six thinking hats: An essential approach to business management.* New York, NY: Little, Brown, & Company.

Deci, E. L. (1975). *Intrinsic motivation.* New York: Plenum.

Deci, E. L. & Ryan, R. M. (1985). *Intrinsic motivation and self-determination in human behavior.* New York: Plenum Press.

Deci, E. L. & Ryan, R. M. (2000). The "what" and "why" of goal pursuits: Human needs and the self-determination of behavior. *Psychological Inquiry, 11*(4), 227–268.

Deci, E. L. & Ryan, R. M. (Eds.). (2002). *Handbook of self-determination research.* Rochester: The University of Rochester.

Deci, E. L., Ryan, R. M., Gagné, M., Leone, D. R., Usunov, J., & Kornazheva, B. P. (2001). Need satisfaction, motivation, and well-being in the work organizations of a former eastern bloc country. *Personality and Social Psychology Bulletin, 27*(8), 930–942.

Dilts, R. (1990). *Changing belief systems with NLP.* Cupertino: Meta Publications.

Elliot, A. J., McGregor, H. A., & Trash, T. M. (2002). The need for competence. In E. L. Deci & R. M. Ryan (Eds.), *Handbook of self-determination research* (pp. 361–387). Rochester: The University of Rochester Press.

Enthoven, M. (2007). *The ability to bounce beyond.* Pretoria, South Africa: University of Pretoria.

Epstein, S. (1998a). Cognitive-experiential self-theory: A dual-process personality theory with implications for diagnosis and psychotherapy. In R. F. Bornstein & J. M. Masling (Eds.), *Empirical perspectives on the psychoanalytic unconscious* (pp. 99–140). Washington, DC: APA.

Epstein, S. (1998b). *Constructive thinking, the key to emotional intelligence.* Westport, CT: Praeger.

Epstein, S. (1990). Cognitive-experiential self-theory. In L. A. Pervin (Ed.), *Handbook of personality, theory and research* (pp. 165–192). New York: The Guilford Press.

Fiske, S. T. & Taylor, S. E. (1991). *Social cognition.* New York: McGraw-Hill.

Fredrickson, B. L. (1998). What good are positive emotions? *Review of General Psychology, 2*(3), 300–319.

Fredrickson, B. L. (2001). The role of positive emotions in positive psychology: The broaden-and-build theory of positive emotions. *American Psychologist, 56*(3), 218–226.

Fredrickson, B. L. (2002). Positive emotions. In C. R. Snyder & S. J. Lopez (Eds.), *Handbook of positive psychology* (pp. 120–134). Oxford: Oxford University Press.

Fredrickson, B. (2009). *Positivity: Groundbreaking research reveals how to embrace the hidden strength of positive emotions, overcome negativity, and thrive.* New York: Random House.

Fredrickson, B. L. (2013, July 15). Updated thinking on the positivity ratios. *American Psychologist, 68*(9), 814–822.

Fredrickson, B. L. & Losada, M. L. (2005). Positive affect and the complex dynamics of human flourishing. *American Psychologist, 60,* 678–686.

Friborg, O., Hjemdal, O., Martinussen, M., & Rosenvinge, J. H. (2009). Empirical support for resilience as more than the counterpart and absence of vulnerability and symptoms of mental disorder. *Journal of Individual Differences, 30*(3), 138–151.

Garland, E. L., Fredrickson, B., Kring, A. M., Johnson, D. P., Meyer, P. S., & Penn, D. L. (2010). Upward spirals of positive emotions counter downward spirals of negativity: Insights from the Broaden-and-Build Theory and affective neuroscience on the treatment of emotion dysfunctions and deficits in psychopathology. *Clinical Psychology Review, 30*(7), 849–864.

Gegenfurtner, A., Veermans, K., Festner, D., & Gruber, H. (2009). Motivation to transfer training: An integrative literature review. *Human Resource Development Review, 8*(3), 403–423.

Greene, M. (1973). *Teacher as stranger.* Belmont, CA: Wadsworth.

Hamachek, D. (1999). Effective teachers: What they do, how they do it, and the importance of self-knowledge. In R. P. Lipka & T. M. Brinthaupt (Eds.), *The role of self in teacher development* (pp. 189–224). Albany, NY: State University of New York Press.

Hansen, D. T. (1995). *The call to teach.* New York: Teachers College Press.

Hodgins, H. S. & Knee, C. R. (2002). The integrating self and conscious experience. In E. L. Deci & R. M. Ryan (Eds.), *Handbook of self-determination research* (pp. 87–100). Rochester: The University of Rochester Press.

Hodgins, H. S., Koestner, R., & Duncan, N. (1996). On the compatibility of autonomy and relatedness. *Personality and Social Psychology Bulletin, 22*(3), 227–237.

Hoekstra, A. (2007). *Experienced teachers' informal learning in the workplace.* Utrecht, Netherlands: Utrecht University.

Hoekstra, A. & Korthagen, F. A. J. (2011). Teacher learning in a context of educational change: Informal learning versus systematic support. *Journal of Teacher Education, 62*(1), 76–92.

Hoekstra, A. & Korthagen, F. A. J. (2013). Coaching based on core reflection makes a difference. In F. A. J. Korthagen, Y. M. Kim, & W. L. Greene (Eds.), *Teaching and learning from within: A core reflection approach to quality and inspiration in education* (pp. 93–107). New York/London: Routledge.

Immordino-Yang, M. H. & Damasio, A. (2007). We feel, therefore we learn: The relevance of affective and social neuroscience to education. *Mind, Brain and Education, 1*(1), 3–10.

Intrator, S. M. & Kunzman, S. (2006). Starting with soul. *Educational Leadership*, March 2006, 38–42.

Järvilehto, T. (2001). Feeling as knowing – Part 2. Emotion, consciousness, and brain activity. *Consciousness & Emotion, 2*(1), 75–102.

Kabat-Zinn, J. (1990). *Full catastrophe living: Using the wisdom of your body and mind to face stress, pain, and illness.* New York: Delacourt.

Kasser, T. (2002). Sketches for a self-determination theory of values. In E. L. Deci & R. M. Ryan (Eds.), *Handbook of self-determination research* (pp. 123–140). Rochester: The University of Rochester Press.

Kelchtermans, G. & Vandenberghe, R. (1994). Teachers' professional development: A biographical perspective. *Journal of Curriculum Studies, 26*, 45–62.

Kim, Y. M. & Greene, W. L. (2013). Aligning professional and personal identities: Applying core reflection in teacher education practice. In F. A. J. Korthagen, Y. M. Kim, & W. L. Greene (Eds.), *Teaching and learning from within: A core reflection approach to quality and inspiration in education* (pp. 165–178). New York/London: Routledge.

Kim, H., Chan, H. C., & Chan, Y. P. (2007). A balanced thinking–feelings model of information systems continuance. *International Journal of Human-Computer Studies, 65*, 511–525.

King, J. T. & Lau-Smith, J. (2013). Teaching form the inside out: Discovering and developing the self-that-teaches. In F. A. J. Korthagen, Y. M. Kim, & W. L. Greene, *Teaching and learning from within: A core reflection approach to quality and inspiration in education* (pp. 47–60). New York/London: Routledge.

Klein, S. B., Rozendal, K., & Cosmides, L. (2002). A social-cognitive neuroscience analysis of the self. *Social Cognition, 20*(2), 105–135.

Korthagen, F. A. J. (2004). In search of the essence of a good teacher: Towards a more holistic approach in teacher education. *Teaching and Teacher Education, 20*(1), 77–97.

Korthagen, F. A. J. (2010a). Going to the core: Deepening reflection by connecting the person to the profession. In N. Lyons (Ed.), *Handbook of reflection and reflective inquiry: Mapping a way of knowing for professional reflective inquiry* (pp. 529–552). New York: Springer.

Korthagen, F. A. J. (2010b). Teacher reflection: What it is and what it does. In E. G. Pultorak (Ed.), *The purposes, practices, and professionalism of teacher reflectivity: Insights for twenty-first-century teachers and students.* Lanham, ML: Rowman & Littlefield.

Korthagen, F. A. J. (2010c). How teacher education can make a difference. *Journal of Education for Teaching, 36*(4), 407–423.

Korthagen, F. A. J. & Kessels, J. P. A. M. (1999). Linking theory and practice: Changing the pedagogy of teacher education. *Educational Researcher, 28*(4), 4–17.

Korthagen, F. & Lagerwerf, B. (2001). Teachers' professional learning: how does it work? In F. A. J. Korthagen, J. Kessels, B. Koster, B. Lagerwerf, & T. Wubbels, T., *Linking practice and theory: The pedagogy of realistic teacher education* (pp. 175–206). Mahwah, NJ: Lawrence Erlbaum Associates.

Korthagen, F. & Vasalos, A. (2005). Levels in reflection: Core reflection as a means to enhance professional development. *Teachers and Teaching: Theory and Practice, 11*(1), 47–71.

Korthagen, F. A. J., Kessels, J., Koster, B., Lagerwerf, B., & Wubbels, T. (2001). *Linking practice and theory: The pedagogy of realistic teacher education.* Mahwah, NJ: Lawrence Erlbaum Associates.

Korthagen, F. A. J., Kim, Y. M., & Greene, W. L. (Eds.). (2013). *Teaching and learning from within: A core reflection approach to quality and inspiration in education.* New York/London: Routledge.

Koster, B., Korthagen, F. A. J., & Schrijnemakers, H. G. M. (1995). Between entry and exit: How student teachers change their educational values under the influence of teacher education. In F. Buffet & J. A. Tschoumy (Eds.), *Choc démocratique et formation des enseignants en Europe* (pp. 156–168). Lyon: Presses Universitaires de Lyon.

Krishnamurti, J. (1991). *The collected works of J. Krishnamurti, Volume XI (1958–1960).* Ojai, CA: The Krishnamurti Foundation of America.

La Guardia, J. G. & Ryan, R. M. (2007). Why identities fluctuate: Variability in traits as a function of situational variations in autonomy support. *Journal of Personality, 75*, 1205–1228.

Luthans, F., Youssef, C. M., & Avolio, B. J. (2007). *Psychological capital: Developing the human competitive edge.* Oxford/New York: Oxford University Press.

Mansvelder-Longayroux, D., Beijaard, D., & Verloop, N. (2007). The portfolio as a tool for stimulating reflection by student teachers. *Teaching and Teacher Education, 23*(1), 47–62.

Marotto, M., Roos, J., & Victor, B. (2007). Collective virtuosity in organizations: A study of peak performance in an orchestra. *Journal of Management Studies 44*(3), 388–413.

Masten, A. S. & Reed, M. J. (2002). Resilience in development. In C. R. Snyder & S. Lopez (Eds.), *Handbook of positive psychology* (pp. 74–88). Oxford: Oxford University Press.

Mayes, C. (2001). A transpersonal model for teacher reflectivity. *Journal of Curriculum Studies, 33*(4), 477–493.

McLean, S. V. (1999). Becoming a teacher: The person in the process. In R. P. Lipka & T. M. Brinthaupt (Eds.), *The role of self in teacher development* (pp. 55–91). Albany, NY: State University of New York Press.

Meijer, P. C., Korthagen, F. A. J., & Vasalos, A. (2009). Supporting presence in teacher education: The connection between the personal and professional aspects of teaching. *Teaching and Teacher Education, 25*(2), 297–308.

Meijer, P. C., Korthagen, F. A. J., & Vasalos, A. (2013). Coaching based on core reflection: A case study on supporting presence in teacher education. In F. A. J. Korthagen, Y. M. Kim, & W. L. Greene, *Teaching and learning from within: A core reflection approach to quality and inspiration in education* (pp. 76–92). New York/London: Routledge.

Milanese, N., Iani, C., & Rubichi, S. (2010). Shared learning shapes human performance: Transfer effects in task sharing. *Cognition 116*(1), 15–22.

Newman, C. S. (2000). Seeds of professional development in pre-service teachers: A study of their dreams and goals. *International Journal of Educational Research, 33*(2), 125–217.

Noddings, N. (1984). *Caring: A feminine approach to ethics and moral education.* Berkeley: University of California Press.

Ofman, D. (2000). *Core qualities: A gateway to human resources.* Schiedam: Scriptum.

Ossebaard, M., Korthagen, F. A. J., Oost, H., Stavenga-De Jong, J., & Vasalos, A. (2013). A core reflection approach to reducing study procrastination. In F. A. J. Korthagen, Y. M. Kim, & W. L. Greene, *Teaching and learning from within: A core reflection approach to quality and inspiration in education* (pp. 148–161). New York/London: Routledge.

Palmer, P. J. (1998). *The courage to teach.* San Francisco, CA: Jossey-Bass.

Pelletier, L. G., Séguin-Lévesque, C., & Legault, L. (2002). Pressure from above and pressure from below as determinants of teachers' motivation and teaching behaviors. *Journal of Educational Psychology, 94*, 186–196.

Peterson, C. & Seligman, M. E. P. (2004). *Character strengths and virtues: A handbook and classification.* Oxford: Oxford University Press.

Poutiatine, M. I. (2009). What is transformation? Nine principles toward an understanding of the transformational process for transformational leadership. *Journal of Transformative Education, 7*(3), 189–208.

Riva, G., Waterworth, J. A.,Waterworth, E. L., & Mantovani, F. (2009). From intention to action: The role of presence. *New Ideas in Psychology, 30*, 1–14.

Rodgers, C. & Raider-Roth, M. (2006). Presence in teaching. *Teachers and Teaching: Theory and Practice, 12*(3), 265–287.

Ruit, P. & Korthagen, F. A. J. (2013). Developing core qualities in young students. In F. A. J. Korthagen, Y. M. Kim, & W. L. Greene, *Teaching and learning from within: A core reflection approach to quality and inspiration in education* (pp. 131–147). New York/London: Routledge.

Russell, J. A. (1980). A circumplex model of affect. *Journal of Personality and Social psychology, 39*(6), 1161–1178.

Ryan, R. M. (1995). Psychological needs and the facilitation of integrative processes. *Journal of Personality, 63*(3), 397–427.

Ryan, R. M. & Deci, E. L. (2000a). The darker and brighter sides of human existence: Basic psychological needs as a unifying concept. *Psychological Inquiry, 11*(4), 319–338.

Ryan, R. M. & Deci, E. L. (2000b). Self-determination theory and the facilitation of intrinsic motivation, social development, and well-being. *American Psychologist, 55*(1), 68–78.

Ryan, R. M. & Deci, E. L. (2001). On happiness and human potentials: A review of research on hedonic and eudaimonic well-being. *Annual Review of Psychology, 52*, 141–166.

Ryan, R. M. & Deci, E. L. (2002). Overview of Self-Determination Theory: An organismic dialectical perspective. In E. L. Deci & R. M. Ryan (Eds.), *Handbook of self-determination research* (pp. 3–33). Rochester: The University of Rochester.

Ryan, R. M., Kuhl, J., & Deci, E. L. (1997). Nature and autonomy: An organizational view of social and neurobiological aspects of self-regulation in behavior and development. *Development and Psychopathology, 9*, 701–728.

Ryan, R. M., Sheldon, K., Kasser, T., & Deci, E. L. (1996). All goals are not created equal: An organismic perspective on the nature of goals and their regulation. In P. M. Gollwitzer & J. A. Bargh (Eds.), *The psychology of action: Linking cognition and motivation to behaviour* (pp. 7–26). New York: Guilford.

Scharmer, C. O. (2007). *Theory U: Leading from the future as it emerges.* Cambridge, MA: Society for Organizational Learning.

Schön, D. A. (1987). *Educating the reflective practitioner.* San Francisco, CA: Jossey-Bass.

Seligman, M. E. P. (2002). Positive psychology, positive prevention, and positive therapy. In C. J. Snyder & S. J. Lopez (Eds.), *Handbook of positive psychology* (pp. 3–12). New York: Oxford University Press.

Seligman, M. E. P. (2003). *Authentic happiness: Using the new positive psychology to realize your potential for lasting fulfillment.* London: Nicholas Brealey Publishing.

Seligman, M. E. P. & Csikszentmihalyi, M. (2000). Positive psychology: An introduction. *American Psychologist, 55*(1), 5–14.

Seligman, M. E. P. & Peterson, C. (2003). Positive clinical psychology. In L. G. Aspinwall & U. M. Staudinger (Eds.), *A psychology of human strengths: Fundamental questions and future directions for a positive psychology.* Washington, DC: APA.

Seligman, M. E. P., Steen, T., Park, N., & Peterson, C. (2005). Positive psychology progress: Empirical validation of interventions. *American Psychologist, 60*(5), 410–421.

Senge, P., Scharmer, C. O., Jaworski, J., & Flowers, B. S. (2004). *Presence: Exploring profound change in people, organizations and society.* London: Nicolas Brealey Publishing.

Shani, Y., Tykocinski, O. E., & Zeelenberg, M. (2008). When ignorance is not bliss: How feelings of discomfort promote the search for negative information. *Journal of Economic Psychology, 29*, 643–653.

Sheldon, K. M. (2002). The self-concordant model of healthy goal striving: When personal goals correctly represent the person. In E. L. Deci & R. M. Ryan (Eds.), *Handbook of self-determination research* (pp. 65–86). Rochester: The University of Rochester Press.

Sheldon, K. M. & Bettencourt, B. A. (2002). Psychological needs and subjective well-being in social groups. *British Journal of Social Psychology, 41*, 25–38.

Sheldon, K. M. & Elliot, A. J. (1999). Goal striving, need satisfaction, and longitudinal well-being: The self-concordant model. *Journal of Personal and Social Psychology, 76*(3), 482–497.

Sheldon, K. M. & Houser-Marko, L. (2001). Self-concordance, goal attainment, and the pursuit of happiness: Can there be an upward spiral? *Journal of Personal and Social Psychology, 80*(1), 152–165.

Sheldon, K. M. & Kasser, T. (2001). Goals, congruence, and positive well-being: New empirical support for humanistic theories. *Journal of Humanistic Psychology, 41*(1), 30–50.

Simon, K. G. (2001). *Moral questions in the classroom: How to get kids to think deeply about real life and their schoolwork.* New Haven, CT: Yale.

Skinner, E. & Edge, K. (2002). Self-determination, coping, and development. In E. L. Deci & R. M. Ryan (Eds.), *Handbook of self-determination research* (pp. 297–337). Rochester: The University of Rochester Press.

Taylor, S. E., Kemeny, M. E., Reed, G. M., Bower, J. E., & Gruenewald, T. L. (2000). Psychological resources, positive illusions, and health. *American Psychologist, 55*, 99–109.

Thrash, T. M. & Elliot, A. J. (2003). Inspiration as a psychological construct. *Journal of Personality and Social Psychology, 84*(4), 871–889.

Thrash, T. M. & Elliot, A. J. (2004). Inspiration: Core characteristics, component processes, antecedents, and function. *Journal of Personality and Social Psychology, 87*(6), 957–973.

Thrash, T. M., Elliot, A. J., Maruskin, L. A., & Cassidy, S. E. (2010a). Inspiration and the promotion of well-being: Tests of causality and mediation. *Journal of Personality and Social Psychology, 98*(3), 488–506.

Thrash, T. M., Maruskin, L. A., Cassidy, S. E., Fryer, J. W., & Ryan, R. M. (2010b). Mediating between the muse and the masses: Inspiration and the actualization of creative ideas. *Journal of Personality and Social Psychology, 98*(3), 469–487.

Tsaousis, I., Nikolaou, I., Serdaris, N., & Judge, T. A. (2007). Do the core self-evaluations moderate the relationship between subjective well-being and physical and psychological health? *Personality and Individual Differences, 42*, 1441–1452.

Tugade, M. M. & Fredrickson, B. L. (2004). Resilient individuals use positive emotions to bounce back from negative emotional experiences. *Journal of Personality and Social Psychology, 86*(2), 320–333.

Tusin, L. F. (1999). Deciding to teach. In R. P. Lipka & T. M. Brinthaupt (Eds.), *The role of self in teacher development* (pp. 11–35). Albany, NY: State University of New York Press.

Vallerand, R. J., Blanchard, C., Mageau, G. A., Koestner, R., Ratelle, C., Leonard, M., Gagné, M., & Marsolais. J. (2003). Les passions de l'ame: On obsessive and harmonious passion. *Journal of Personality and Social Psychology, 85*(4), 756–767.

Van Woerkom, M. (2003). *Critical reflection at work: Bridging individual and organisational learning.* Enschede, Netherlands: Universiteit Twente.

Webb, T. L. & Sheeran. P. (2006). Does changing behavioral intentions engender behavior change? A meta-analysis of the experimental evidence. *Psychological Bulletin, 132*(2), 249–268.

Wegner, D. M. & Wheatley, T. (1999). Apparent mental causation: Sources of the experience of will. *American Psychologist, 54*(7), 480–492.

Wegner, D. M. & Wheatley, T. (2003). The mind's best trick: How we experience conscious will. *Trends in Cognitive Sciences, 7*(2), 65–69.

Weinstein, N., Brown, K. W., & Ryan, R. M. (2009). A multi-method examination of the effects of mindfulness on stress attribution, coping, and emotional well-being. *Journal of Research in Personality, 43,* 374–385.

Wenger, E. (1998). *Communities of practice: Learning, meaning, and identity.* Cambridge: Cambridge University Press.

About the Authors

Frits G. Evelein is an international speaker and trainer in cooperative and co-creative teaching and learning. He has published various books in this field. He is currently developing an educational pedagogy that is based on new insights into consciousness. In addition, he is active as a composer and participates in the creation of multimedia projects. Previously, Frits has worked as a music teacher and professor of teacher education in the Netherlands, both at Utrecht University and Codarts University of Performing Arts.
E-mail: f.g.evelein@gmail.com

Fred A. J. Korthagen has been a mathematics teacher and a teacher educator. In 2000, he became a professor of teacher education at Utrecht University, the Netherlands. He specializes in the professional development of teachers and teacher educators. He is a co-developer of the core reflection approach and has worked with many schools, both national and international, on the use of this approach. He received international awards for his scientific work, for example from the American Association of Teacher Educators (ATE) and the American Educational Research Association (AERA).
E-mail: fred@korthagen.nl

Overview of Website Materials to Accompany this Book @ www.routledge.com/9780415819961

Cards	Number of cards	Activities
1. Core qualities pictures	24	4
2. Using the elevator	24	24, 75, 76
3. Using the elevator (short version)	12	24, 75, 76
4. Using the elevator: Ask a question about . . .	12	24, 75, 76
5. Ideals	24	36
6. Core qualities	24	5, 6, 7, 8, 9, 10, 12, 13, 25, 37, 46, 47, 75, 76
7. Core qualities in action	16	11
8. Body	8	50, 51, 52, 61
9. Roles	16	63
10. Environment, identity, and core qualities	8	64
11. Constructive beliefs	16	61
12. Destructive beliefs	16	60
13. Downloading	8	71
14. Being in touch versus drifting	8	69

Figures	Activities
15. Three types of core qualities (Figure 2.2)	5
16. The elevator (Figure 3.1)	24
17. Feeling quadrants (Figure 3.2)	22
18. The scale of wanting (Figure 3.3)	25
19. The flow model (Figure 5.1)	45
20. The elaborate flow model (Figure 5.2)	45, 47
21. The onion model (Figure 7.1)	54
22. The beliefs scale (Figure 7.3)	60
23. Card for increasing presence and mindfulness (Figure 8.1)	72
24. The core reflection model (Figure 9.1)	77, 78
25. How to place the core reflection sheets (Figure 9.2)	77, 78

Tables	Activities
26. Feeling words (Table 3.1)	22
27. Basic needs satisfaction at work questionnaire (Table 4.1)	29
28. Mindfulness questionnaire (Table 8.1)	72
29. Guidelines for coaching using core reflection (Table 9.1)	77, 78

Forms	Activities
30. Feeling quadrants form (Figure 3.2)	22
31. Comparing four feelings form	23
32. Thinking, feeling, and wanting placemats	24, 74, 75
33. Core reflection placemats	77, 78

Index